BEST MOVIES OF THE 80S

Portable Press
An imprint of Printers Row Publishing Group
10350 Barnes Canyon Road, Suite 100, San Diego, CA 92121
www.portablepress.com • e-mail: mail@portablepress.com

Printers Row Publishing Group is a division of Readerlink Distribution
Services, LLC. Portable Press is a registered trademark of Readerlink
Distribution Services, LLC.

All notations of errors or omissions should be addressed to Portable Press,
Editorial Department, at the above address. All other correspondence
(author inquiries, permissions) concerning the content of this book should
be addressed to www.carltonbooks.co.uk.

For Portable Press:
Publisher: Peter Norton
Associate Publisher: Ana Parker
Publishing/Editorial Team: Vicki Jaeger, Lauren Taniguchi
Editorial Team: JoAnn Padgett, Melinda Allman, Dan Mansfield

For Carlton Books:
Project Editor: Ross Hamilton
Design: Katie Baxendale
Production: Emily Noto
Picture Research: Steve Behan

Library of Congress Cataloging-in-Publication Data available on request.

ISBN: 978-1-68412-573-9

Printed in Dubai

22 21 20 19 18   1 2 3 4 5

BEST MOVIES OF THE 80S

HELEN O'HARA

PORTABLE PRESS

San Diego, California

CONTENTS

INTRODUCTION

DECADES LATER, AND THE 1980S CONTINUE TO EXERCISE AN OUTSIZE INFLUENCE ON OUR CULTURE.

The music is still referenced, the fashions keep threatening to come back, and even the hairstyles won't stay completely dead (much as we might want them to). The same is particularly true of the decade's movies. The names of most big 1980s blockbuster movies are familiar even to those who were not yet born when the films were released—and their stars are still working, sometimes in the same franchises.

Directors such as Steven Spielberg, James Cameron, and Tim Burton continue to reign supreme, and many of the A-list directors who have followed them—such as J. J. Abrams and David Fincher—have dipped their toes into sequels or reboots of 1980s movies. In fact, seven movies on this list have sparked (or suffered) reboots; twenty-eight have had sequels; and yet more have launched prequels, television spin-offs, or stage musicals. Their influence on our world today is out of all proportion to their age, and shows no sign of diminishing. The generation that grew up in the 1980s adored their movies and introduced them to their kids as the acme of entertainment. But what is it about 1980s pop culture that makes it unique?

It's worth looking at the time that gave it birth. The old Hollywood studio machine had broken down by the late 1960s, unable to keep up with the rise in popularity of television or properly absorb the countercultural spirit of the age. In its place rose a wealth of new, independent-minded moviemakers who pushed film in directions that television couldn't match. Moviemaking in the late 1960s and early 1970s moved toward the darker

or more transgressive likes of *Bonnie and Clyde, The Graduate,* and *Taxi Driver* or toward the more epic—but still adult—movies tackling the kind of story that television wouldn't attempt until the 2000s; think of *The Godfather* and *Apocalypse Now.*

Many of these movies were made by the "movie brats," the first generation of moviemakers to have grown up with a mature movie industry to watch. They had studied film as an art form instead of earning their stripes in theater or within the studio system. This group—including Francis Ford Coppola, Martin Scorsese, Steven Spielberg, George Lucas, John Milius, and Brian De Palma—changed the way movies were made, layering in allusions to earlier moviemakers they admired and pushing the art in new directions. In the second half of the 1970s, as the oil crisis died down and the global economy began to perk up, these moviemakers reinvented what success looked like for studios, particularly with the knockout punches that were *Jaws, Close Encounters of the Third Kind,* and *Star Wars.* There had been "blockbuster" movies before, but *Jaws* began the "blockbuster era," where every studio executive aimed to make the biggest movie of all time each time they went to bat. They wanted to make movies that were wildly popular and unlike anything you'd seen before. That quest would shape the 1980s.

The name of the game was half a billion dollars worldwide, a barrier that *E.T.* would smash in 1983. *Close Encounters* and *Star Wars* made it clear that science fiction and other fantastical tales had a particularly high chance of breaking out worldwide, so the 1980s became a golden age for sci-fi invention.

Right: In his role as the cocksure fighter pilot Maverick, Tom Cruise gave the 1980s one of its quintessential heroes.

Left: *The Empire Strikes Back* upped the ante from *A New Hope* to become that rarest of things: a blockbuster sequel that's better than the original.

Above: In a decade overflowing with tank top–wearing action heroes, Bruce Willis's John McClane managed to stand out in *Die Hard*.

Top: A manic and knife-wielding Glenn Close attacks Michael Douglas in one of *Fatal Attraction*'s most thrilling and disturbing scenes.

Meanwhile, producers such as Don Simpson, Jerry Bruckheimer, and Joel Silver more or less invented the modern action movie, proving that you didn't need to shoot aliens to thrill people, and cemented the "high-concept" thriller as a cultural mainstay with movies such as *Lethal Weapon*, *Die Hard*, and *Top Gun*. However, the more adult successes of the 1970s lingered, too, allowing for great horror, from *The Thing* to *Fatal Attraction*, and modern morality tales, from *Wall Street* to *Scarface*.

Over in Chicago, John Hughes almost single-handedly saved the teen movie from irrelevance, while a fallow period of creative stagnancy at Walt Disney Animation led to a new and wider explosion of talent as trained animators sought opportunities elsewhere (Tim Burton, Don Bluth, and John Lasseter struck out from Disney with great success), while a few hardy souls fought to revive the Mouse House's animation legacy by the decade's end with *The Little Mermaid* and *Who Framed Roger Rabbit*.

It was a time of change, of innovation, and of something like hope. While many cinema purists will still argue for the supremacy of the art form in the 1970s, with its reputation for taking risks and gritty realism, the wild, populist experimentation of the 1980s has had more effect on what most of us watch now, for good or bad. These big, brash movies changed the world, influencing Hong Kong cinema, Japanese animation, and Bollywood as well as directing and shaping the making of Western movies.

So, this is a celebration of those days—and the movies that still inspire fond memories. But before you read further, a few caveats. You're bound to disagree with at least some of the movies I've chosen, especially because I've focused on mainstream American movies. I faced some difficult choices when trying to balance contemporary success at the time of release, enduring influence, and importance to the genre. I rejected a few movies on the basis that they didn't feel sufficiently 1980s. That meant saying goodbye to favorite period dramas such

Right: The British are coming— *Chariots of Fire*'s tale of athletes in search of Olympic glory turned out to be an Academy darling.

as *The Untouchables* and *Amadeus* (*Chariots of Fire* survives almost entirely on the basis of that Vangelis theme). But it also meant turning down movies at each end of the decade that felt more properly part of the 1970s or 1990s. *Raging Bull* feels like a piece of Scorsese's earlier work, while (at the other end of the decade) *Bill & Ted's Excellent Adventure* feels quintessentially 1990s. I know—most heinous.

The list is also overwhelmingly male, straight, and white. For the most part, there was little other choice in a book designed to cover the most widely loved and influential movies of the decade, because white male leads and creators predominate the movies that were seen to such a huge degree. I have tried to call out the worst cases of sexism, racism, and other prejudices in their plots, but the list itself is a testament to privilege. Hopefully, the selection at least shows that society has moved on since then, although a similar selection of the past ten years would feature many of the same stars and directors.

This list also includes a few movies that are, objectively, not great. That's because I've tried to select the movies that are most representative of the 1980s rather than simply listing the finest movies made during that decade. *Highlander*, for instance, remains ridiculous, but something about its spirit seems to capture the decade in which it's set, so it won a place in this book.

I have tried to atone for at least some of my omissions by placing more greats in the "Further Viewing" recommendations in each movie section, as well as some of my own favorites that didn't make the cut. These selections are linked to the movie they accompany by having a shared director or star, by theme or genre or, in one case, by composer. I hope that you'll find some treasures in here as well as on the main list.

Finally, and most importantly, I hope that you enjoy this nostalgia trip. It's a treat to revisit a decade that was exuberant, self-confident to an absurd degree, and filled with young, daring moviemakers taking extraordinary risks. If you are moved to go back and reassess an old favorite or try out a movie that you missed, I think you will be glad you did. For all their limitations in effects, in representation, and in sensitivity, the best movies of the 1980s are still funny and weird and wildly entertaining.

HELEN O'HARA

Opposite: In a decade of bizarre genre movies, *Highlander* might be the strangest of all.

Left: Perhaps the most iconic single shot in all of 1980s cinema, this scene from *E.T.* has even come to be featured on the logo of Spielberg's Amblin Entertainment.

1980 HIGHLIGHTS

The decade began as audiences were chilled by *The Shining*, Stanley Kubrick's horror masterpiece, and thrilled by *Star Wars: The Empire Strikes Back*. Robert De Niro and Martin Scorsese set a new standard for visceral filmmaking in *Raging Bull*, while Michael Cimino's career faltered after the disastrous reception of *Heaven's Gate*.

HIGHEST-GROSSING FILMS (U.S.)

1. *The Empire Strikes Back*	20th Century Fox	$209,398,025
2. *Nine to Five*	20th Century Fox	$103,290,500
3. *Stir Crazy*	Columbia	$101,300,000
4. *Airplane!*	Paramount	$83,453,539
5. *Any Which Way You Can*	Warner Bros.	$70,687,344
6. *Private Benjamin*	Warner Bros.	$69,847,348
7. *Coal Miner's Daughter*	Universal	$67,182,787
8. *Smokey and the Bandit II*	Universal	$66,132,626
9. *The Blue Lagoon*	Columbia	$58,853,106
10. *The Blues Brothers*	Universal	$57,229,890

AT THE GOLDEN GLOBES

Best Picture (Drama) — *Ordinary People*

Best Picture (Comedy/Musical) — *Coal Miner's Daughter*

Best Director — Robert Redford, *Ordinary People*

Best Actor (Drama) — Robert De Niro, *Raging Bull*

Best Actor (Comedy/Musical) — Ray Sharkey, *The Idolmaker*

Best Actress (Drama) — Mary Tyler Moore, *Ordinary People*

Best Actress (Comedy/Musical) — Sissy Spacek, *Coal Miner's Daughter*

CANNES FILM FESTIVAL

Palme d'Or winner

All That Jazz, Bob Fosse

Kagemusha, Akira Kurosawa (tie)

NOTABLE DEATHS

Alfred Hitchcock, April 29 — Director, *Psycho*, *Rear Window*, and *Vertigo*

Peter Sellers, July 24 — Actor, *The Pink Panther* and *Dr. Strangelove*

Steve McQueen, November 7 — Actor, *The Great Escape* and *Bullitt*

Mae West, November 22 — Playwright and actor, *She Done Him Wrong* and *I'm No Angel*

John Lennon, December 8 — Musician and actor, *A Hard Day's Night* and *Yellow Submarine*

AT THE OSCARS

Best Picture — *Ordinary People*

Best Director — Robert Redford, *Ordinary People*

Best Actor — Robert De Niro, *Raging Bull*

Best Actress — Sissy Spacek, *Coal Miner's Daughter*

THIS YEAR'S BIG OSCARS INJUSTICE

Martin Scorsese's *Raging Bull* was overlooked, beyond De Niro's award. The director would have to wait until 2006's *The Departed* for his long-overdue Best Director statuette.

FUTURE MOVIE STAR BIRTHS

February 12: Christina Ricci, *The Addams Family* and *Sleepy Hollow*

April 26: Channing Tatum, *Magic Mike* and *21 Jump Street*

July 18: Kristen Bell, *Frozen* and *The Good Place*

August 26: Chris Pine, *Star Trek* and *Hell or High Water*

November 12: Ryan Gosling, *The Notebook* and *La La Land*

NOTABLE FILM DEBUTS

Michelle Pfeiffer, *The Hollywood Knights*

Tom Hanks, *He Knows You're Alone*

Pierce Brosnan, *The Long Good Friday*

Michael J. Fox, *Midnight Madness*

Sharon Stone, *Stardust Memories*

Bruce Willis, *The First Deadly Sin*

THE EMPIRE STRIKES BACK & RETURN OF THE JEDI

HOW DO YOU FOLLOW UP THE BIGGEST MOVIE OF ALL TIME? IT'S NOT A QUESTION THAT MANY FILMMAKERS HAVE HAD TO CONTEND WITH.

But George Lucas has, and he surely felt some sense of trepidation as he faced the prospect of continuing the story of *Star Wars Episode IV: A New Hope*, a film that redefined what movies could do, a movie that drew in people who hadn't been to a movie theater in decades. Then again, Lucas had always modeled his space opera on the sci-fi serials of the 1930s, so there was some kind of road map to follow. No one could have guessed, however, just how good the sequels would be.

The Empire Strikes Back (1980) is still, nearly forty years later, generally accepted as the best movie in the franchise. It takes the characters and world established in *A New Hope* and makes them bigger, darker, and deeper. It's a cliché to say that a sequel will be darker, but Lucas's success with *Empire* is a big part of the reason why going dark became so ubiquitous. *Empire* sees our heroes fighting for their lives in the spectacular land battle on Hoth that begins the movie, and then split up for most of the running time. Luke (Mark Hamill) receives a mystical message from his deceased mentor and travels to Dagobah to train as a Jedi with the impish Master Yoda (Frank Oz and one of the all-time great puppets). Meanwhile, Han (Harrison Ford) and Leia (Carrie Fisher) narrowly escape the Empire a bunch of times, admit they are insanely attracted to one another, and are betrayed in Cloud City by Han's old buddy Lando Calrissian (Billy Dee

Williams). It's bigger, more emotionally complex, and far more dramatic than the film that came before it, but *Empire* is still full of the envelope-pushing effects, silly humor, and big action that had defined *A New Hope*.

And then there's that twist, much imitated but never bettered. It's hard to remember how seismic that revelation was ("No. *I* am your father.") in an age before internet spoilers and obsessive production stories. The idea that Vader was a good man corrupted to the dark side of the Force gave weight to Yoda and Obi-Wan Kenobi's warnings about the Force, and it added danger to Luke's exploration of his abilities. Suddenly, he was not just a farm boy toying with magic; he was at risk of losing his very soul to the worst people in the galaxy in return for power. And the wrong choice could cost his friends their lives.

Of course, Luke manages to resist Vader, bringing us to *Return of the Jedi* in 1983. The third installment of the original trilogy gets a bad rap from fans, but it features some of the best scenes of the entire trilogy and a stunning final act, crosscutting between another dogfight in space, a land struggle between vastly unequal forces, and another personal duel where Luke is both warrior and prize.

This time, after a quick stop at Jabba's palace on Tatooine to rescue Han from his carbonite prison and take out the galaxy's most feared gangster, the Rebels have to destroy another Death Star, while Luke must face down Vader and his boss, Emperor Palpatine (Iain McDiarmid), once and for all. The mission takes them to the forest moon of Endor and its indigenous race of low-tech, highly cute teddy bears, the Ewoks. Fans now like to pretend they hated the Ewoks even as kids, but c'mon—these critters were genetically engineered to be irresistible. They are also tougher than they're given credit for. Created as an explicit nod to the Viet Cong, they take down a technologically superior force with wiliness and some clever logging.

And above them, in the stars, Luke fights for his own soul, and his father's, and that of his sister Leia. He prevails, of course, but there's a bittersweet note to the triumph here, a sense of something lost as well

as won. It's that final tinge of maturity and an uncertain future that would sustain the *Star Wars* fandom through the next three decades, through years without any movies and years with disappointing efforts. Lucas, for all his faults as a scripter of dialogue and a lover of technical dazzle, created something truly extraordinary with these first three movies, something that has become a part of our collective cultural DNA and has colored every sequel that followed them.

Left: C3PO (Anthony Daniels), Princess Leia (Carrie Fisher), and Han Solo (Harrison Ford) in the cockpit of the *Millennium Falcon*. Han has a bad feeling about something.

Right: Luke Skywalker (Mark Hamill), with a blaster by his side.

ORIGINAL RELEASE DATE:
Empire, June 20, 1980 (U.S.); May 20, 1980 (UK)
Jedi, May 25, 1983 (U.S.); June 2, 1983 (UK)
RUN TIME: 124 minutes; 131 minutes

DID YOU KNOW?

◆ The Lucasfilm computer division's Graphics Group, created in 1979 to work on *Empire*, would be spun off and eventually became Pixar Animation.

FURTHER VIEWING

◆ *Spaceballs* (1987)
What better way to understand the full impact of *Star Wars* than by watching this spoof, starring John Candy as a Chewbacca-like half-man/half-dog and John Hurt reprising his big *Alien* scene?

FACTS

THE BLUES BROTHERS

1980

ONE OF THE MOST EXPENSIVE COMEDIES EVER MADE AT THE TIME, *THE BLUES BROTHERS* CAUGHT ITS STARS, JOHN BELUSHI AND DAN AYKROYD, AT THE HEIGHT OF THEIR *SATURDAY NIGHT LIVE*–BORN TELEVISION FAME, AND ITS DIRECTOR, JOHN LANDIS, NEAR THE HEIGHT OF HIS POWERS.

It redefined how insanely good movie soundtracks could get and how insanely over the top movie car crashes could be, and—like its titular musicians—it duly thumbed its nose at authority and did exactly as it liked.

We join Jake Blues (Belushi) on his release from prison, although we don't see his face until he's shed his prison duds for a suit and hat, backlit by the setting sun as if he has descended from heaven. After he reunites with his adoptive brother Elwood (Aykroyd), a scary nun (Kathleen Freeman) gives them the task of raising $5,000 to pay back taxes on the orphanage where they were reared. Doing so will require putting on a charity concert, which requires getting the band back together, which involves a madcap journey all over Illinois. In pursuit of their mission, they commit felonies, play country music, and receive divine inspiration, overseen by James Brown as a fiery preacher. Angry country musicians, seemingly every car in Illinois's law-enforcement community, and, of course, some Illinois Nazis (which seemed such a nonsensical concept in 1980) pursue the Blues Brothers.

Aykroyd and Belushi had performed the Blues Brothers as cast members on *Saturday Night Live*, so they had honed their schtick and knew that the characters worked. The plot was a little trickier: Aykroyd's initial script was far too long (he'd never written one before and wrote a booklike treatise, including character backstory and other

unnecessary detail), and director John Landis had to significantly redraft it with only weeks to go. Filming began without an approved budget, but that was okay, because Landis and his stars blew past the budget without pausing. Belushi, who died of a drug overdose in 1982, was partying hard at this stage in

Below: Jake (John Belushi, right) and Elwood Blues (Dan Aykroyd, left) are on a mission from God to save an orphanage—by any means necessary.

his career, adding delays and difficulties to the work, and Landis faced steady studio criticism over his choice of cast and extravagant stunt requirements. He crashed 103 cars for the outrageous final chase scene—a record that wasn't broken until 1998's belated sequel *Blues Brothers 2000* trashed 104—and closed downtown Chicago and the Daley Center for the finale, at a cost of a then-astronomical $3.5 million. In one of the funniest depictions of wild police overreaction ever put on film ("Use of excessive force has been approved," announces one police radio operator), 500 extras dressed as cops, National Guardsmen, firefighters, and FBI all stormed about the city.

This is, of course, a movie about soul music led by two white guys and directed by another. But they're clearly also music aficionados, gazing adoringly at their cameoing musical legends and letting them take center stage. To his credit, Landis had to fight to include every one of them against a studio that saw them as has-beens and wanted younger, bigger names—and his fight paid off. The film gave Aretha Franklin, Ray Charles, John Lee Hooker, and James Brown a chance to sing on the big screen, and introduced Cotton Club legend Cab Calloway to a new and younger audience, reviving the careers of every one of them.

The stunts are spectacular, from an opening bridge leap to that final all-car pileup. The beautiful Helen of Troy may have launched a thousand ships, but Jake and Elwood managed about the same number of Cadillacs and Chevys, and neither is a looker. And it's a great film for cameos: Frank Oz and Steven Spielberg appear as minor functionaries, while Carrie Fisher (Aykroyd's girlfriend at the time) has a hilarious recurring role as Jake's vengeful ex-fiancée.

Through it all sail Jake and Elwood, largely nonplussed by what's happening around them. During a wildly destructive chase through a mall, they casually comment on the stores that have recently opened, and they don't even bother mentioning it when the Illinois Nazis start shooting at them. These two are men of the world, and it takes more than a few bullets or an exploding building to worry them—although they do take a solemn

moment when their Bluesmobile spontaneously falls to pieces. The movie ends with the entire band in prison performing—what else?—"Jailhouse Rock" and sparking a prison riot. Even there, the power of soul music can't be contained. No matter how many armed guards are thrown at them, you can't stop this beat.

Below: Elwood and Jake in front of the Bluesmobile, the former police car that led Illinois's law-enforcement community on a merry chase.

ORIGINAL RELEASE DATE: June 20, 1980 (U.S.); October 10, 1980 (UK)
RUN TIME: 142 minutes

DID YOU KNOW?

◆ The name "Blues Brothers" was suggested to Aykroyd and Belushi by Howard Shore, then a fixture at the head of *SNL*'s house band. He would go on to become a movie composer and score, among others, *The Lord of the Rings*.

FURTHER VIEWING

◆ *Spies Like Us* (1985)
After Belushi's death, Aykroyd had success pairing with Chevy Chase in this story of two hapless government employees who become convinced that they are key U.S. spies.

FACTS

"IT'S 106 MILES TO CHICAGO. WE'VE GOT A FULL TANK OF GAS, HALF A PACKET OF CIGARETTES, IT'S DARK, AND WE'RE WEARING SUNGLASSES."

Elwood Blues (Dan Aykroyd), *THE BLUES BROTHERS*

THE 1980S IN MOVIE TAGLINES

There are a few different ways to make a memorable tagline. The best ones tell you just enough about a film's story to make you want to know more, ideally in a witty way (for example, *Back to the Future*). A few rely on word play (*Cocktail*) or weird humor (*Fast Times . . .*). And one line here has almost nothing to do with its movie (*The Fly*)—but it still became iconic. Go figure.

"IF NANCY DOESN'T WAKE UP SCREAMING, SHE WON'T WAKE UP AT ALL."

A NIGHTMARE ON ELM STREET, 1984

"THEY'LL NEVER GET CAUGHT. THEY'RE ON A MISSION FROM GOD."

THE BLUES BROTHERS, 1980

"MAN HAS MADE HIS MATCH . . . NOW IT'S HIS PROBLEM."

BLADE RUNNER, 1982

"HE IS AFRAID. HE IS ALONE. HE IS THREE MILLION LIGHT-YEARS FROM HOME."

E. T. THE EXTRA-TERRESTRIAL, 1982

"FAST CARS. FAST GIRLS. FAST CARROTS. FAST CARROTS?"

FAST TIMES AT RIDGEMONT HIGH, 1982

"SCIENCE CREATED HIM. NOW CHUCK NORRIS MUST DESTROY HIM."

SILENT RAGE, 1982

"MAN IS THE WARMEST PLACE TO HIDE."

THE THING, 1982

"IT'S TIME FOR THE ODDS TO GET EVEN."

REVENGE OF THE NERDS, 1984

"HE WAS NEVER IN TIME FOR HIS CLASSES . . . HE WASN'T IN TIME FOR HIS DINNER . . . THEN ONE DAY . . . HE WASN'T IN HIS TIME AT ALL."

BACK TO THE FUTURE, 1985

"HERBERT WEST HAS A VERY GOOD HEAD ON HIS SHOULDERS . . . AND ANOTHER ONE IN A DISH ON HIS DESK."

RE-ANIMATOR, 1985

"BE AFRAID. BE VERY AFRAID."

THE FLY, 1985

AIRPLANE!

1980

A STRONG CONTENDER FOR THE FUNNIEST MOVIE OF ALL TIME, AS LONG AS YOUR TASTES RUN TO THE SERIOUSLY SILLY, *AIRPLANE!* PACKS 223 GAGS INTO 84 MINUTES.

That's more than 2.6 jokes per minute, including sight gags and that postcredit sting ("I'll give him another ten minutes"), and it is a rare moviegoer who doesn't laugh at something. The three directors—Jerry Zucker, Jim Abrahams, and David Zucker—screen-tested their movie to within an inch of its life, touring college campuses and ruthlessly cutting anything that didn't get a big laugh. The result is a potent mix of smart and wacky jokes, wrapped around an unlikely disaster movie framework.

The plot and even some of the dialogue were lifted wholesale from 1957's *Zero Hour* to the extent that the ZAZ team bought the rights to remake that film when they began work on their own. They thought that *Zero Hour* had an ideal structure, and although they'd written a lot of sketch comedy (as shown in their previous effort as writers, *Kentucky Fried Movie*), they were nervous about structuring an entire movie from scratch. Even some of the names are the same. Our hero Ted Striker (Stryker in the original), played by Robert Hays, is a veteran pilot who has been left traumatized by the loss of his men during a covert war mission. But when, on a flight to reconnect with the estranged love of his life, the pilot and copilot become ill, Ted is the only one who can land the plane and save the passengers.

Perhaps Abrahams and the Zuckers didn't need to worry so much about structure, because it's not as if any of the story really matters. *Airplane!*'s effect is all about the glorious nonsequiturs, ridiculous wordplay, and unlikely casting. It's about serious people facing sky-high stakes, only to respond by straight-facedly doing ludicrous things. The stroke of genius that made it possible was the decision by Abrahams and the Zuckers to cast serious actors instead of comedians, so that the film looks and feels just like the disaster

Left: Elaine (Julie Hagerty), Randy (Lorna Patterson), Dr. Rumack (Leslie Nielsen) and Captain Clarence Oveur (Peter Graves) in the cockpit of the stricken passenger jet.

my drinking problem" before tossing water over his shoulder when he attempts to knock back a glass; keep an eye on the little girl whose IV tube is dislodged by the singing nun; and marvel at the way that Barbara "June Cleaver" Billingsley shows up as a sweet, white-haired old lady who can speak jive ("Jive ass dude don't got no brains anyhow"). Ethel Merman plays a traumatized soldier convinced he's Ethel Merman; basketball legend Kareem Abdul-Jabbar plays copilot Roger Murdock ("Roger, Roger. What's our vector, Victor?") but somehow also himself, because why not?

By any logical, reasonable standard, *Airplane!* should be a mess, but logic and reason have no place here. This is a movie that has been carefully engineered to keep you watching and make you laugh a lot—and nothing else. As such, it's an elegant beast, a comedy powerful enough to launch a whole subgenre—the "spoof," which went on to further glory with *Top Secret, Police Squad*, and the rest before the *Scary Movie* series killed it—and one that continues to provoke helpless giggles. Surely no one can resist it. Just don't call it Shirley.

movies that inspired it—right up until it goes off the rails. Robert Stack, Peter Graves, Leslie Nielsen, and Lloyd Bridges were established, midlevel Hollywood stars of respectable pedigree, and the directors encouraged them to keep their faces straight and their reactions tightly controlled. The results were far funnier than they could have been in the hands of long-term clowns. Two of the standout stars—Nielsen and Bridges—would find a whole new career path as a result of their work here, going on to star in the likes of *The Naked Gun, Police Squad*, and *Hot Shots!* Roger Ebert dubbed Nielsen "the Laurence Olivier of spoofs," and the former star of *The Forbidden Planet* and *The Poseidon Adventure* finished the last three decades of his career as a comedy star. Not bad for a low-budget movie from first-time directors.

However, it's the jokes that are the real star here. There are the repeated groaners that somehow get funnier with repetition ("The cockpit! What is it?"; "Well, it's a little room at the front of the plane . . . ") and the elaborate re-creations of well-loved movies (*Saturday Night Fever, Airport 1975*). There are the carefully planned one-liners ("Give me Ham on 5; hold the Mayo.") and the moments of bad-taste shock humor ("Joey, do you like movies about gladiators?"). Even the throwaway gags are golden. Listen to the way that Striker delivers the line "That's when I developed

FACTS

ORIGINAL RELEASE DATE:
July 2, 1980 (U.S.); August 7, 1980 (UK)
RUN TIME: 84 minutes

DID YOU KNOW?

- The voices delivering the "white zone" and "red zone" loudspeaker announcements in the movie were by the same two people who recorded the real Los Angeles International announcements at the time. Their bickering characters are in a relationship; the pair was also married in real life.

FURTHER VIEWING

- *Top Secret* (1984)
  The Naked Gun is good, but the insane spy thrills of *Top Secret* are better. A young Val Kilmer stars as Elvis-like Nick Rivers, who is caught up in an espionage plot of surpassing silliness.

NINE TO FIVE

1980

ANYONE WHO HAS EVER WORKED IN AN OFFICE, MALE OR FEMALE, CAN IDENTIFY WITH SOMETHING IN *NINE TO FIVE*.

Left: Fonda, Tomlin, Parton, and Coleman sporting some very bouffant hairdos in the promo poster image for *Nine to Five*.

But the boss who passes one worker over for promotion, sexually harasses another, and unfairly threatens to fire a third is a particular nightmare for women, for whom such figures are still all too familiar. So this cheerful story of three secretaries who set out to get revenge on the manager from hell still feels remarkably like wish fulfillment.

We enter the world of Consolidated Companies alongside Jane Fonda's Judy Bernly, prim and nervous in pastels. She's taking her first steps into professional work after a nasty divorce, because her husband, unsubtly called Dick (Lawrence Pressman), ran off with his assistant. Judy is mentored by supervisor Violet (Lily Tomlin), who's frustrated by endless cases of the men she trains being promoted past her. One of those who leapfrogged past her is their boss, the awful Franklin Hart Jr. (Dabney Coleman), who is openly sexist toward his female employees. Worse, he wages a steady war of sexual harassment against his personal secretary Doralee (Dolly Parton) and spreads lies around the office that she's sleeping with him, so that she is ostracized by the other workers. However, after a particularly bad day reveals the truth, the three start working together.

They get drunk, and then stoned, and each fantasizes about the way they'd like to take Hart down. Judy imagines a mob, complete with torches, hunting Mr. Hart through the office, until she takes over with a shotgun. Doralee imagines being a sexist cowgirl boss who harasses him right back, while Violet dreams of turning into Snow White and poisoning his coffee—a Disney princess we've never seen before. But when, the next day, Violet thinks that she has accidentally poisoned Mr. Hart and he learns about it—thanks to tattletale Roz (Elizabeth Wilson)—he tries to coerce Doralee into sex in return for his silence. She ties him up and they hold him hostage for several weeks, planning to blackmail him in turn for his embezzlement, and they engage in a little reeducation of the boss.

"You're a sexist, egotistical, lying, hypocritical bigot," says Judy.

"So I have a few flaws; who doesn't?" answers Hart, indignant.

Perfectly fizzy chemistry between the three female leads keeps even the sillier scenes (stealing a body from a hospital) ticking along, and it's good to see Judy and Doralee stand up for themselves (Tomlin's Violet, of course, always could). Fonda conceived the idea for the movie and produced it, bringing screenwriter Patricia Resnick in to craft a story that portrayed workplace sexism without being preachy about it. Fonda also recruited director Colin Higgins, who did a more comic pass on the script, and Tomlin and Parton, the latter for her first film role. Fonda wanted the story to explain that "You can run an office without a boss, but you can't run an office without the secretaries!"

The story convincingly demonstrates that point, with the three women nimbly covering for their boss's absence and instituting any number of woman-friendly policies behind his back. They set up a crèche, allow flexible working hours, and create a job-sharing plan for those who can't work full time. Productivity soars—and Hart returns, discombobulated, to find himself credited with the lot.

Still, this is an odd movie. The extended hospital heist, where the women end up with a stranger's corpse in the back of Violet's car, is a weird diversion from the main story, and the whole last act feels a little confused. The women's long-cooking plan to blackmail Hart for his embezzlement deflates like a bad soufflé, and they're rescued from charges of kidnapping only when he is promoted to a new post . . . in Brazil. Fonda was so anxious to avoid any appearance of hectoring the viewer with strong leftist positions on women in the workplace that some of the message is almost buried in a rush to the ending, and it's only your genuine affection for these women, and the laughs along the way, that keep it all together.

At least we learn, through the credits, that Violet finally gets her promotion, Judy finds a new husband, and Hart is kidnapped by a remote tribe of Amazons. And Doralee? She goes off to become a country music star. Someone must have heard her song about office life. The best movie theme of the 1980s is a hotly contested title, but this one has got to be in with a shot. That catchy tune and superb lyrics make it almost as relatable as this story itself.

ORIGINAL RELEASE DATE: December 19, 1980 (U.S.); March 27, 1981 (UK)
RUN TIME: 107 minutes

DID YOU KNOW?

- The typewriter sound on the song "9 to 5" is in fact Dolly Parton clicking her false nails together.

FURTHER VIEWING

- *Steel Magnolias* (1989)
  For another female-led movie starring Dolly Parton, look no further than this tearjerker, with an all-star cast including Sally Field, Shirley MacLaine, Olympia Dukakis, Daryl Hannah, and Julia Roberts.

FACTS

1981 HIGHLIGHTS

Raiders of the Lost Ark redefined the action blockbuster in the summer of 1981, but its closest challenger at the U.S. box office was a sedate drama starring two elderly icons. Screenwriter Colin Welland announced that "The British are coming" as *Chariots of Fire* swept the Oscars, and *Rebel Without a Cause* star Natalie Wood died tragically at sea off Catalina Island.

HIGHEST-GROSSING FILMS (U.S.)

1. *Raiders of the Lost Ark*	Paramount	$212,222,025
2. *On Golden Pond*	Universal	$119,285,432
3. *Superman II*	Warner Bros.	$108,185,706
4. *Arthur*	Orion Pictures / Warner Bros.	$95,461,682
5. *Stripes*	Columbia	$85,297,000
6. *The Cannonball Run*	20th Century Fox	$72,179,579
7. *Chariots of Fire*	Warner Bros.	$58,972,904
8. *For Your Eyes Only*	United Artists	$54,812,802
9. *The Four Seasons*	Universal	$50,427,646
10. *Time Bandits*	Embassy Pictures	$42,365,581

AT THE GOLDEN GLOBES

Best Picture (Drama)   *On Golden Pond*

Best Picture (Comedy/Musical)   *Arthur*

Best Director   Warren Beatty, *Reds*

Best Actor (Drama)   Henry Fonda, *On Golden Pond*

Best Actor (Comedy/Musical)   Dudley Moore, *Arthur*

Best Actress (Drama)   Meryl Streep, *The French Lieutenant's Woman*

Best Actress (Comedy/Musical)   Bernadette Peters, *Pennies from Heaven*

CANNES FILM FESTIVAL

Palme d'Or winner

Man of Iron, Andrzej Wajda

NOTABLE DEATHS

William Wyler, July 27   Director, *Ben-Hur* and *Roman Holiday*

Paddy Chayefsky, August 1   Screenwriter, *Network* and *Marty*

Anita Loos, August 18   Screenwriter and author, *Gentlemen Prefer Blondes* and *Red-Headed Woman*

Gloria Grahame, October 5   Actor, *The Bad and the Beautiful* and *The Big Heat*

Natalie Wood, November 29   Actor, *Rebel Without a Cause* and *West Side Story*

AT THE OSCARS

Best Picture   *Chariots of Fire*

Best Director   Warren Beatty, *Reds*

Best Actor   Henry Fonda, *On Golden Pond*

Best Actress   Katharine Hepburn, *On Golden Pond*

THIS YEAR'S BIG OSCARS INJUSTICE

Raiders of the Lost Ark is the best film and best achievement in directing of the year, but it was never going to be an Oscar darling. At least it was nominated.

FUTURE MOVIE STAR BIRTHS

January 28: Elijah Wood, *The Lord of the Rings* trilogy and *Everything Is Fine*

February 9: Tom Hiddleston, *Thor* and *High Rise*

June 9: Natalie Portman, *Leon: The Professional* and *Black Swan*

June 13: Chris Evans, *Captain America* and *Snowpiercer*

September 4: Beyoncé, *Dreamgirls* and *The Lion King*

NOTABLE FILM DEBUTS

Ben Affleck, *The Dark End of the Street*

Kim Basinger, *Hard Country*

Tom Cruise, *Endless Love*

Meg Ryan, *Rich and Famous*

Kathleen Turner, *Body Heat*

RAIDERS OF THE LOST ARK

1981

ONE OF THE BIGGEST HITS OF THE 1980S WAS A PASTICHE OF MOVIE SERIALS FROM THE 1930S, VIA THE COPYCAT COMICS AND TV SERIES OF THE 1950S THAT ITS TWO CREATORS HAD GROWN UP ON. NO WONDER IT HAS PROVED TIMELESS.

Producer George Lucas and director Steven Spielberg famously conceived the idea for Indiana Jones on a vacation in Hawaii, watching Lucas's dog Indiana galloping about the beach ("We named the dog Indiana!" sulks Sean Connery's Henry Jones Sr. in *The Last Crusade*). They still remembered those childhood adventure stories of explorers fondly. Why not introduce them to a whole new audience?

That vacation musing turned into a movie that is practically perfect. *Raiders of the Lost Ark* updated the often-shaky effects of the movies that inspired it and recruited the greatest stuntmen in the business. Instead of a California desert, Spielberg and crew went to North Africa and employed proper locations and hundreds of extras. The script was zingy, the romance reminiscent of the great screwball banter of *Bringing Up Baby*, and the stakes, literally, biblical.

But the real key was finding the right Indiana Jones. Tom Selleck famously auditioned, and was offered the role before his commitment to *Magnum PI* prevented him from taking it, and Tim Matheson came close. But despite Lucas's reluctance to repeat his *Star Wars* casting, there was only one choice as the world's worst archaeologist and greatest movie hero. Harrison Ford brought sardonic wit, an edge of self-awareness, and a gift for comic timing that made Indiana Jones an immediate hit. In that first outing, the supporting cast was equally inspired. Karen Allen's Marion was the perfectly spunky foil to his hangdog hero and Paul Freeman's Belloq is one of the great faux-genteel villains.

The importance of Spielberg's inspired touch was never better felt than here. There's the fake-out, where a Nazi pulls a terrifying torture device from inside his leather jacket, only to reveal that it's a hanger for his coat. The swordsman in the bazaar engaging in a dazzling display of skill until Indy simply shoots him. (Famously, this was originally a lengthy whip/sword duel trimmed, because both star and director had food poisoning.) The Nazi monkey,

Above: In one of the all-time great opening scenes, Dr. Henry "Indiana" Jones (Harrison Ford) outruns a massive boulder in a booby-trapped South American tomb.

Left: Drew Struzan's glorious poster, recalling the 1930s adventure classics that inspired Spielberg and Lucas.

Indy's dad worked, even if in actuality he is only twelve years older than Ford. Lately, however, the compass has swung the other way: *Doom*'s hard edges have been embraced and its bravery acknowledged, and those weird flourishes (Cole Porter in Mandarin? Sure!) accepted as seasoning. The movie's cultural insensitivity has aged less well, admittedly, but there's meat on its bones. *The Last Crusade*, meanwhile, came to seem a little contrived and patronizing. Its witty prologue, which explains all Indy's quirks—from snake phobia to scarred chin—and with River Phoenix as the young Henry Jones Jr., has become the model for the inevitable origin story in every modern movie franchise, and its reputation has suffered from association with all those lesser incarnations.

The fact is that both of the later 1980s Indiana Jones movies are better than we have any right to expect, filled with excitement and terror and the thrill of learning new things. And *Raiders* remains practically perfect in every way. If adventure has a name, as the tagline to *Temple of Doom* said, it must be Indiana Jones.

poisoned dates, and snake-infested Egyptian ruins offered the same familiar beats we'd read in *Tintin* or watched in those old adventure stories, but taken just a little bit further and funnier—or scarier—than we'd seen before.

Indy screws up far more often than he succeeds, and there's a fair argument that, had he sat out the events of *Raiders* entirely, the outcome would have been much the same. The Nazis still would have been fried by the wrath of God, and the Ark still left unusable by Hitler. However, the point is not how often he fails, but how hard he tries to do the right thing. He is a profoundly human hero, and that's something that was, mercifully, sustained through the prequel and sequel that followed.

Fan opinion seesaws on the follow-ups *The Temple of Doom* and *The Last Crusade*. At the time, *Doom* was held as a byword for a disappointing sequel, a darker and more twisted follow-up with a less satisfying love story, while *Last Crusade* was considered more satisfying and closer in tone to the original. Certainly, the addition of Sean Connery as

ORIGINAL RELEASE DATE: June 12, 1981 (U.S.); July 30, 1981 (UK)
RUN TIME: 115 minutes

DID YOU KNOW?
- There weren't enough snakes in England for the Well of Souls sequence, so Spielberg had a hose cut to the right length and scattered around the set.

FURTHER VIEWING
- *Romancing the Stone* (1984)
  Robert Zemeckis's Indy, ahem, tribute—established the Michael Douglas/Kathleen Turner pairing that would power three films, and remains one of the best rom-coms of the decade.

FACTS

MTV & MOVIES

LAUNCHED ON AUGUST 1, 1981, MUSIC TELEVISION SOON PLAYED A CRUCIAL ROLE IN 1980S CULTURE.

By playing music videos all day, every day—interspersed with "video jockey" introductory segments—the channel made music a more image-conscious, visually inventive art form. Fashions became wilder and the videos became steadily more cinematic, driven by the likes of Michael Jackson's epic "Thriller" video (directed by John Landis) and A-Ha's animated classic for "Take on Me."

But MTV also appeared in the movies themselves. In *The Lost Boys*, Corey Haim's Sam has one big complaint when he moves to Santa Clara: no TV.

"Do you know what it means when there's no TV? No MTV!" A similar disaster strikes in *Spies Like Us*, where Dan Aykroyd and Chevy Chase's hapless bumbling leads to the destruction of the MTV satellite, and far worse in *A Nightmare on Elm Street 4: The Dream Master*, when Joey (Rodney Eastman) falls asleep while watching the channel and becomes victim to Freddy Krueger.

Despite poor Joey's experience, the channel became a mark of cool for teens of the era. So Ferris Bueller (Matthew Broderick) watches it before

he starts his day off, Sarah Jessica Parker's NASA intern watches it in *Flight of the Navigator*, and tough older brother Brand (Josh Brolin) keeps an eye on it as he works out in *The Goonies*. It endures, rather presciently, for decades into the future in *Back to the Future Part II*, and even features on Blaine's T-shirt in *Predator*.

Within just a few years of its founding, MTV had changed film. The likes of *Top Gun*, *Footloose*, and *Flashdance* used the signature rapid cuts and stylized editing of the channel's music videos, and music video directors, such as David Fincher and Michael Bay, took over Hollywood. The channel's slogan said "*Turn it on. Leave it on.*" Hollywood listened.

Left: Prince made a film called *Purple Rain* to tie in with his album of the same name. Semi-autobiographical and packed with concert footage, it brought in about ten times its budget at the box office.

Opposite: Madonna's "Like a Prayer" video caused controversy, since it tells the story of a girl (Madonna) who witnesses a white supremacist murder, hides in a church, and prays to God for the courage to bear witness.

1982 HIGHLIGHTS

Four all-time great science-fiction films were released this summer, and while *E.T.* was the undisputed box-office champion, *The Wrath of Khan*, *Blade Runner*, and *The Thing* would prove just as influential on the genre. At the Oscars, Meryl Streep won her first Best Actress prize and *Gandhi* proved just as powerful onscreen as he had been in reality.

HIGHEST-GROSSING FILMS (U.S.)

1. *E.T. the Extra-Terrestrial*	Universal	$359,197,037
2. *Tootsie*	Columbia	$177,200,000
3. *An Officer and a Gentleman*	Paramount	$129,795,554
4. *Rocky III*	United Artists	$124,146,897
5. *Porky's*	20th Century Fox	$105,492,483
6. *Star Trek II: The Wrath of Khan*	Paramount	$78,912,963
7. *48 Hrs.*	Paramount	$78,868,508
8. *Poltergeist*	Metro-Goldwyn-Mayer	$76,606,280
9. *The Best Little Whorehouse in Texas*	Universal	$69,701,637
10. *Annie*	Columbia	$57,059,003

AT THE GOLDEN GLOBES

Best Picture (Drama) — *E.T. the Extra-Terrestrial*

Best Picture (Comedy/Musical) — *Tootsie*

Best Director — Richard Attenborough, *Gandhi*

Best Actor (Drama) — Ben Kingsley, *Gandhi*

Best Actor (Comedy/Musical) — Dustin Hoffman, *Tootsie*

Best Actress (Drama) — Meryl Streep, *Sophie's Choice*

Best Actress (Comedy/Musical) — Julie Andrews, *Victor/Victoria*

CANNES FILM FESTIVAL

Palme d'Or winner

Missing, Costa Gavros

NOTABLE DEATHS

John Belushi, March 5 — Actor, *Animal House* and *The Blues Brothers*

Henry Fonda, August 12 — Actor, *12 Angry Men* and *The Grapes of Wrath*

Ingrid Bergman, August 29 — Actor, *Casablanca* and *Notorious*

Grace Kelly, September 14 — Actor, *Rear Window* and *To Catch a Thief*

Jacques Tati, November 5 — Actor, *Jour de fête* and *Mon Oncle*

AT THE OSCARS

Best Picture — *Gandhi*

Best Director — Richard Attenborough, *Gandhi*

Best Actor — Ben Kingsley, *Gandhi*

Best Actress — Meryl Streep, *Sophie's Choice*

THIS YEAR'S BIG OSCARS INJUSTICE

This was a startlingly strong year, particularly in the Best Director category, and while *Gandhi's* scale was overwhelming, Richard Attenborough's achievement has endured less well than Spielberg's *E.T.*, Wolfgang Petersen's *Das Boot*, Sidney Lumet's *The Verdict*, or Sydney Pollack's *Tootsie*.

FUTURE MOVIE STAR BIRTHS

January 6: Eddie Redmayne, *The Theory of Everything* and *The Danish Girl*

March 22: Constance Wu *Crazy Rich Asians* and *Fresh Off the Boat*

April 5: Hayley Atwell, *Captain America: The First Avenger* and *Brideshead Revisited*

April 15: Seth Rogen, *Superbad* and *This Is the End*

November 12: Anne Hathaway, *Les Misérables* and *The Dark Knight Rises*

NOTABLE FILM DEBUTS

Nicolas Cage, *Fast Times at Ridgemont High*

Glenn Close, *The World According to Garp*

Jet Li, *Shaolin Temple*

Angelina Jolie, *Lookin' to Get Out*

Eddie Murphy, *48 Hrs.*

CHARIOTS OF FIRE

1982

NOT EVERY OSCAR WINNER—NOT EVEN MOST—PASSES INTO POPULAR CULTURE IN THE WAY THAT *CHARIOTS OF FIRE* DID.

Although few people could tell you the specifics of its story, huge numbers know the Vangelis-composed theme, and know that it accompanies slow-motion running. And when accepting his Academy Award for Best Screenplay, writer Colin Welland cheered that "The British are coming!"—which wasn't quite true for the underperforming British film industry in the 1980s, but managed to pass into movie legend anyway.

The movie is a story about athletics, specifically the British track team at the 1924 Olympics. After a flash-forward to the 1978 funeral of one of our heroes, we take up the story in 1919, immediately after World War I, with the UK still reeling from the loss of a generation of young men. In this atmosphere, a new crop of students, some of them war veterans, arrive at Caius College in Cambridge and join the running team.

Ben Cross is the intense Henry Abrahams. While at college, Abrahams becomes the first man to complete the "Trinity Great Court Run" around the college quad, swiftly followed by Nigel Havers's Lord Andrew Lindsay. Running coach Sam Mussabini (Ian Holm) starts to work with him on the 100 meters, reassuring him, "A short sprint is run on nerves. It's tailor-made for neurotics." Under his determination and sometimes arrogance, it's fear and insecurity that powers Abrahams, as well as anger against the anti-Semites he has had to face his whole life amid the British upper crust. "I don't run to take beatings! I run to win. If I can't win, I won't run." Abrahams is out to show the whole world that he's as good as them.

Meanwhile in Scotland, the devout Eric Liddell (Ian Charleson) is also drawing attention for his speed, which is met with disapproval from his puritanical sister Jennie (Cheryl Campbell). Eric is charming,

Above: Abrahams (left) and Lindsay (right) attempt the Great Court Run.

Opposite: The famous opening beach scene was filmed along West Sands beach in St. Andrews, Scotland.

subject matter, with Vangelis's score—a rival with *Blade Runner* for his best work—a modern touch that keeps the film from feeling overly cute.

For most of the running time, the characters embody the British stiff upper lip, but this hits emotional notes when it wants—such as in the scene showing Sam, who as a professional coach is not allowed into the Olympic stadium, celebrating alone—and there are deep threads of friendship underneath the competition. When Liddell gets his gold without compromising his principles, it's one of the great triumphant moments in sports movies. And although a lot of the history was shifted in time or location (Nigel Havers's character was a lightly fictionalized figure, and Nicholas Farrell's Aubrey Montague went to Oxford, not Cambridge), the bones of the story were all there.

The movie won four Oscars, including Best Picture, Screenplay, and Score. It was a generous result for the Academy, given that the U.S. team is the heroes' biggest rivals. But more important, it was widely seen and loved, with children in playgrounds mimicking that slo-mo run along the beach at Broadstairs on the east coast of England for years afterward, and endless parodies on television and in films, from *Madagascar* to *Happy Gilmore*. No matter how remote the 1924 Olympics are from today, everyone can identify with that euphoric scene and the absolute joy of movement.

funny, and good with kids, but he subscribes to a strict Christian creed that leads him to hold short sermons after his race meetings. He is satisfied that God would not object to his running career, but there's an uneasiness in Eric himself, as well as in his family, about the fact that he doesn't commit entirely to missionary work. Is his running a proper use of a God-given gift or a distraction from his true work? And Liddell is faced with a serious dilemma when the Olympic heats for his best event are scheduled for a Sunday, his day of rest.

The movie works as powerfully as it does because director Hugh Hudson, producer David Puttnam, and Welland made it a study in contrasts. Both Liddell and Abrahams are fueled by their beliefs, but in wildly different ways. Faith gives Liddell strength from the inside ("So where does the power come from to see the race to its end? From within."). Other characters note that his righteousness carries him through. But religion powers Abrahams from outside, because it has so often been weaponized against him that the anger generated goes straight to his legs. If the movie is nostalgic in its generally positive view of the sportsmanship and the personalities of the runners, it is unstinting in acknowledging the prejudice that Abrahams, for one, faced. Even the music is at odds with the

ORIGINAL RELEASE DATE:
April 9, 1982 (U.S.); May 15, 1981 (UK)
RUN TIME: 121 minutes

DID YOU KNOW?

◆ Future movie star and director Kenneth Branagh had a junior role in the film's production and appears in one scene as a student.

FURTHER VIEWING

◆ *Gandhi* (1982)
Another Oscar-winning historical epic, but on an even larger scale. Richard Attenborough directs Ben Kingsley as Gandhi in a sweeping account of the Mahatma's life, with literally hundreds of thousands of extras.

FACTS

FIRST BLOOD

1982

WHAT IS MOST INTERESTING ABOUT THE FIRST *RAMBO* MOVIE IS WHAT IT IS NOT.

It is not a story that glories in violence or delights in the military prowess of its hero. It is not a pro-America tale about an unstoppable war hero or a mindless excuse to kill loads of people. It is a movie about trauma and close-mindedness and paranoia. No matter how gung-ho the sequels are, *First Blood* is a thoughtful movie that is a tragedy rather than the kind of weightless bloodbath we've seen since, sometimes from the same franchise. "Rambo" may have become a byword for any one-man army, but this original movie is a far smarter, and sadder, beast.

It's based on David Morrell's Vietnam-era novel, about a Vietnam veteran who comes home from the war to find himself treated like one of the hippies who protested against it. A small-town sheriff doesn't like the looks of this drifter and tries to run him out of town, whereupon the former Green Beret reverts to his training and goes to war. The book has a significantly higher body count than the movie, with Rambo slaying about two hundred people. When Stallone came aboard the film and asked to rewrite the script, he removed most of the killing. This Rambo is not directly responsible for any deaths, just a few major woundings and, indirectly, a fall from a helicopter. This lets us sympathize with him and adds to the pathos of his plight.

When we meet Stallone's John J. Rambo, he has wandered up to Washington State in search of his war buddy Delmar Berry. He learns that Delmar died of cancer due to exposure to Agent Orange during the war, and as he walks on up the road into the ironically named town of Hope, he still seems stunned, perhaps grief-stricken. It's in that frame of mind that he is stopped by Sheriff Will Teasle (Brian

Dennehy), one of those law-and-order cops who considers it his mission to apprehend anyone he judges to be poorly dressed. He tries to drive Rambo out of town, and when the vet stubbornly heads back, the sheriff arrests him for "vagrancy, resisting arrest, and carrying a concealed weapon"—a large knife. They beat him up, use a water cannon as a shower, and are about to give him a dry shave when he has a flashback to his time as a POW in Vietnam and freaks out. Rambo punches his way through half the station personnel and escapes to the street, where he steals a dirt bike and makes for the woods.

Once there, John Rambo is unstoppable. A massive manhunt can't capture him, and soon six of the sheriff's deputies have been injured by his improvised booby traps, while another falls from a helicopter while trying to shoot Rambo dead. He holds a knife to Teasle's throat and tells him, "In town you're the law. Out here it's me. Don't push it or I'll give you a war you wouldn't believe." Despite—or perhaps because of—his visible terror, Teasle pushes it.

The only hope for de-escalation comes with the arrival of Colonel Trautman (Richard Crenna), Rambo's wartime commanding officer. He announces himself as the man who "made" the decorated Green Beret, and claims, "I didn't come here to rescue Rambo from you. I came to rescue you from him." But he's been absent too long and can't calm his soldier quickly enough. Rambo disables more men, blows up a gas station and a gun shop, and attacks Teasle at his headquarters before Trautman can talk to him face-to-face.

What happens next is one of those moments that sets this movie apart from its imitators. Rambo breaks down into a rambling speech about his dead comrades in arms and falls crying into the arms of his former CO. This, too, is a change from the book, where Trautman shoots Rambo in the head to end both his rampage and his misery. Here, he lives to fight another day, although he will do so with far less nuanced politics than in this antiwar debut.

The film's first cut came in at over three hours, and Stallone worried that it was career-endingly bad, but director Ted Kotcheff stripped it entirely back

into a propulsive and remarkably effective ninety-minute hit. The dialogue-light, action-heavy, and brilliantly paced result was hugely influential on the action movies that followed (*Predator*, for one, owes it a huge debt). But few of them had the impact that *Rambo* had when it acknowledged the high price of going to war and transforming a man into a perfect killing machine. For all his know-how, Rambo is not an uncomplicated hero.

Opposite: Rambo (Sylvester Stallone) flees a relentless Sheriff Teasle (Brian Dennehy) in an early chase sequence.

Above: Stallone was reportedly horrified with the initial cut of the movie, which ran close to four hours long.

ORIGINAL RELEASE DATE: October 22, 1982 (U.S.); December 12, 1982 (UK)
RUN TIME: 90 minutes

DID YOU KNOW?
◆ Steve McQueen was the first person considered for the role of Rambo back in 1975, but he was judged too old to play a relatively recent Vietnam veteran.

FURTHER VIEWING
◆ *Road House* (1989)
At the other end of the 1980s, Patrick Swayze plays another man trained in violence who is trying to leave all that behind him only for the small town where he's living to decide otherwise. Cue throat-ripping consequences.

FACTS

E.T. THE EXTRA-TERRESTRIAL

1982

THERE IS A FUNDAMENTAL OPTIMISM IN STEVEN SPIELBERG'S OUTLOOK THAT INFORMS ALL HIS MOVIEMAKING—THE IDEA THAT DECENT PEOPLE TRYING TO DO THE RIGHT THING CAN GENERALLY TRIUMPH AGAINST THE ODDS.

But it's never closer to the surface than it was in *E.T.*, the story of a most unlikely friendship that literally spans worlds.

The movie starts by introducing us to young Elliott (the extraordinary Henry Thomas), a child still struggling to adjust to his new reality after his parents' divorce. He discovers something strange living in the garden shed and welcomes it into his home. The thing is a young alien, abandoned during a survey mission to Earth when government goons threatened his whole ship. He's afraid and alone, and Elliott can understand the feeling. The pair learn to communicate with one another and eventually to contact E.T.'s people for help and rescue—while at the same time, Earth authorities hunt for signs of the marooned alien to study and, perhaps, to harm him. Initially, Elliott and E.T. are unaware of the danger, but when they learn of the noose tightening around their lives, they enlist a motley crew of other kids and race toward a magical, musical escape. Their friendship is tentative at first and intense by the end, following a trail of Reese's Pieces from daring connection to a heartbreaking farewell.

There has never been a better collection of child performances than the family in this movie: Henry Thomas's clear-eyed Elliott, Drew Barrymore's indiscreet little sister Gertie, and Robert MacNaughton's bullish older brother Michael. Thomas came into the audition and essentially blew all other contenders away with the ability to cry at

Below: Drew Barrymore's breakout performance was among many highlights of Spielberg's classic.

Below (inset): Elliott (Henry Thomas) and E.T. set off to escape the authorities and return E.T. to his people for the journey home.

and, one senses, a direct stand-in for the director. He wants to know about the universe, and—like Richard Dreyfuss's Roy Neary in *Close Encounters*—has a deep, inexplicable need to see that spaceship at the end. Yet the fact that he doesn't ask for passage, instead standing stunned with his arm around Mary, suggests that the little family may not be fatherless much longer.

It's not a coincidence that, among E.T.'s uncanny powers, is an intense empathetic connection with Elliott. Each feels what the other experiences, from drunkenness to a first kiss (with future *Baywatch* star Erika Eleniak)—and as E.T.'s health fades while he pines for his people, Elliott fades with him. There's a reason that some commentators have drawn comparisons between the little alien, designed to look like a weird mash-up of Einstein and a newborn baby, and Jesus. E.T. has healing, life-giving powers, too, in case you missed the movie's message, and he leaves each of the humans changed by his presence.

Then there is that ending, still devastating nearly forty years later. At the movie's royal premiere in the UK, Princess Diana had to be spirited into the ladies' room to reapply her makeup after the movie finished before she would risk being seen; it reduced even the cynics and hard-bitten art-house fanatics of Cannes to open floods of tears. Spielberg's movie teaches us that the most alien creatures can become our friends if we just open our hearts and that, even if we have to say goodbye forever, we'll always keep them close. That's always going to pack a punch.

will; he would summon up the memory of his recently deceased pet dog and give the movie an emotional impact that remains irresistible. Barrymore is a fourth-generation Hollywood star, and although she knew that E.T. needed a whole troop of people around him to make him move or make noise, as a six-year-old she completely accepted him as a real person. Spielberg, who had already drawn a great performance from Cary Guffey in *Close Encounters of the Third Kind*, channeled the same young-at-heart empathy here to direct them all to utterly convincing turns.

The adults, however, are more important than they're often given credit for. Behind the scenes, master puppeteer Carlo Rambaldi gave E.T. his humanity, turning a wrinkled, squat little creature that even Spielberg described as "something only a mother could love" into everyone's ideal best friend. Meanwhile Spielberg's already established, regular composer John Williams turned in his most emotional score (cue argument from *Star Wars* and *Superman* fans) to make the movie literally soar. And in front of the camera, too, the adults matter. Dee Wallace as Elliott's mother Mary is the picture of a recent divorcee, reeling from self-pity to hard-edged flirtatiousness. The unnamed chief government agent pursuing the alien (Peter Coyote), meanwhile, is obviously at the head of an organization that is a danger to E.T., but his own interest is entirely sincere

Left: The teaser poster riffs on *The Creation of Adam*, Michelangelo's image of God touching fingers with Adam on the ceiling of the Sistine Chapel. And you thought it was just a film about an alien.

ORIGINAL RELEASE DATE: June 11, 1982 (U.S.); December 10, 1982 (UK)
RUN TIME: 114 minutes

DID YOU KNOW?
- Harrison Ford played Elliott's school principal in a scene cut from *E.T.* He was dating screenwriter Melissa Mathison at the time.

FURTHER VIEWING
- *Starman* (1984)
  John Carpenter's sci-fi is sort of *E.T.* played as a romance. Jeff Bridges is the alien who takes the form of Karen Allen's late husband and asks her to drive him across the country.

FACTS

THE SPIELBERG NEXUS

Steven Spielberg directed a number of classic movies in the 1980s, and he shaped many more as a producer and cheerleader for other moviemakers whom he admired. He also launched or boosted the careers of many of the actors he worked with, and, with Hollywood being a small place anyway, he is connected to practically every major movie of the decade.

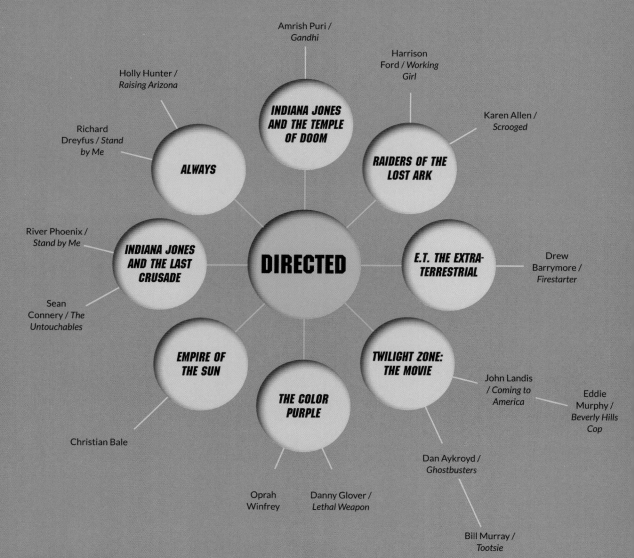

Amrish Puri / *Gandhi*

Harrison Ford / *Working Girl*

Holly Hunter / *Raising Arizona*

Karen Allen / *Scrooged*

Richard Dreyfus / *Stand by Me*

INDIANA JONES AND THE TEMPLE OF DOOM

RAIDERS OF THE LOST ARK

ALWAYS

River Phoenix / *Stand by Me*

DIRECTED

E.T. THE EXTRA-TERRESTRIAL

Drew Barrymore / *Firestarter*

INDIANA JONES AND THE LAST CRUSADE

Sean Connery / *The Untouchables*

EMPIRE OF THE SUN

TWILIGHT ZONE: THE MOVIE

John Landis / *Coming to America*

Eddie Murphy / *Beverly Hills Cop*

THE COLOR PURPLE

Christian Bale

Dan Aykroyd / *Ghostbusters*

Oprah Winfrey

Danny Glover / *Lethal Weapon*

Bill Murray / *Tootsie*

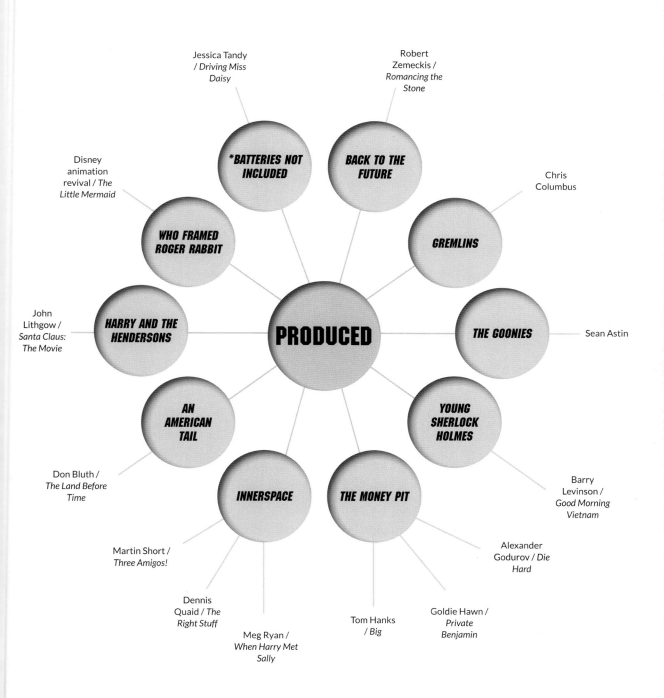

Jessica Tandy / *Driving Miss Daisy*

Robert Zemeckis / *Romancing the Stone*

Disney animation revival / *The Little Mermaid*

Chris Columbus

*BATTERIES NOT INCLUDED

BACK TO THE FUTURE

WHO FRAMED ROGER RABBIT

GREMLINS

John Lithgow / *Santa Claus: The Movie*

HARRY AND THE HENDERSONS

PRODUCED

THE GOONIES

Sean Astin

AN AMERICAN TAIL

YOUNG SHERLOCK HOLMES

Don Bluth / *The Land Before Time*

Barry Levinson / *Good Morning Vietnam*

INNERSPACE

THE MONEY PIT

Martin Short / *Three Amigos!*

Alexander Godurov / *Die Hard*

Dennis Quaid / *The Right Stuff*

Goldie Hawn / *Private Benjamin*

Meg Ryan / *When Harry Met Sally*

Tom Hanks / *Big*

TRON

1982

COMPUTERS: AREN'T THEY BRAND NEW, EXCITING, AND FULL OF LIMITLESS POSSIBILITY? AREN'T THEY ALSO TERRIFYING AND POISED TO TAKE OVER THE WORLD IF WE DON'T WATCH OUT?

Well, yes, apart from the "new" part, which is why *Tron* remains fascinating despite its old-fashioned effects and endless jargon. Director Steven Lisberger started with the concept of telling a story set in a computer and only later added the human bookends to the adventure, and it sometimes shows—but he was ahead of his time with a movie that suggested how much dazzle and excitement computers would one day bring to large-scale moviemaking.

There is a whole lot of exposition before we get to the meat of the story, with two parallel worlds to set up. In the real world, we're introduced to Kevin Flynn (Jeff Bridges), formerly a high-flying computer programmer at ENCOM and now the owner of a games arcade. He worked on game concepts on his corporate computer and his efforts were stolen by Ed Dillinger (David Warner), who used them to secure himself rapid promotions. His colleagues Alan (Bruce Boxleitner) and Dr. Lora Baines (Cindy Morgan) help Flynn get inside ENCOM company headquarters to get proof of Dillinger's theft, while Alan tries to finish work on his *Tron* program upstairs.

Complicating matters is ENCOM's evil "Master Control Program," which blackmails Dillinger for its own ends and plans to infiltrate the Pentagon and Kremlin. Both inside and outside the system, the MCP is blatantly malign and clearly set on expanding its own power to potentially dangerous ends. It uses Lora's invention to zap Flynn into the computer world, where he's forced to fight for his life in gladiatorial-style games against the sadistic Sark (also Warner).

Left: Bruce Boxleitner and Cindy Morgan rendered in timeless 80s-style computer graphics.

The story is a lot to follow, and there's endless technobabble, but some common threads between the worlds help keep track of what's happening. Programs look like their creators, so that Flynn looks like the CLU program he previously created to attempt to infiltrate the MCP from outside, and Tron resembles Alan. At least, after taking a hugely long time to get going, there is fun when Flynn learns he must survive the games and find his way back out into the real world, with the help of Alan's Tron and a Baines avatar called Yori as Tron's love interest. And if Tron and Flynn together can take down the MCP, so much the better.

Understandably, it's not the story that people remember. *Tron* was influential because it was the first movie that made any significant use of computer graphics, and it used them to create a

Left: Syd Mead's light cycles, which even people who haven't seen *Tron* are likely to recognize.

neon-lit, strangely cool world. That's partly due to the director's own tech know-how, but also due to the studio, Disney, bringing in big names to help him. Jean Giraud, aka Moebius, was a hugely influential comic-book artist and futurist, and he designed the extraordinary costumes and most of the system sets, while Syd Mead—who also worked on *Aliens* and *Blade Runner*—designed the vehicles. Even viewers who didn't follow the story still remember the light cycles and those nifty identity disk weapons.

The movie was literally ahead of its time. Alan predicts that, "Some programs will start thinking soon," and ENCOM founder Dr. Gibbs (Barnard Hughes) answers, "Won't that be grand? Computers and programs will start thinking and people will stop." The exchange could come from any tech conference today. The MCP plans to infiltrate the Kremlin and Pentagon to amass more power, which seems all too plausible, and about the only part that remains purely fantastical is the laser that allows Baines to "digitize" organic matter and add it to the system. That gives us the moderately horrific scene where Flynn is erased, piece by piece, to be reconstituted inside the system (the movie doesn't explain why he's restored after the MCP is defeated, but presumably there's a more benevolent ghost somewhere in the machine).

The movie has a belated 2010 sequel, *Tron: Legacy*, which also drew praise for its effects but little for its story. But its true legacy is elsewhere. It galvanized a generation of moviemakers to look carefully at the potential of computer effects, and, in particular, inspired the young animator John Lasseter to experiment with 3-D computer animation at Disney. When his bosses refused to take his project further and fired him, he went on to work with the computer graphics genius Ed Catmull at the Lucasfilm Computer Division, establishing the core partnership that would lead to the foundation of Pixar Studios and animated movies such as *Toy Story*, *Up*, and *Inside Out*. The innovative spirit of *Tron* lives on, outside the computer as well as within.

FACTS

BLADE RUNNER

NO SCIENCE-FICTION MOVIE MADE SINCE *BLADE RUNNER* HAS BEEN FREE OF ITS INFLUENCE.

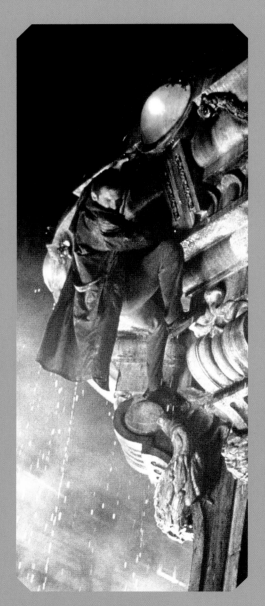

Most have lifted its grungy, lived-in future aesthetic wholesale; a few have deliberately tried to move away from it. But its vision of the future is so immersive that no moviemaker since has been immune, and that's due to the wild source material written by Philip K. Dick—and even more to the genius of Ridley Scott.

It wasn't Scott's first spin at sci-fi, of course; 1979's *Alien* would have been enough to establish him as a master of the genre. But *Blade Runner* went further, envisioning a 2019 Los Angeles of endless night and rain, a city that had cool flying cars and neon-lit ziggurats, but poverty and hustle as well. This was a world away from the shiny futures of the 1960s and 70s, the utopias of *Star Trek* or even the bright white dystopias of *Logan's Run* or *THX-1138*. *Blade Runner* was certainly influenced by the banged-up visions of *Alien* and *Star Wars*, but it offered something more. Instead of silver jumpsuits, this future had retreated to 1940s noir fashions; instead of replicators or "Soylent Green," it had Chinese food and street stalls. It's also a far sexier future than those largely bloodless affairs, although that means it also comes with a healthy side order of misogyny and sexual exploitation, which was carried forward into 2017's equally gorgeous sequel, *Blade Runner 2049*.

But the world-building is only a fraction of its appeal. The plot is twisting and complicated and still a subject of speculation. Deckard is the titular Blade Runner, a kind of officially sanctioned bounty hunter set on the tail of four escaped replicants. These are artificial beings that are advertised as "more human than human," implanted with memories but limited to a four-year life span. The replicants are supposed to work on only the off-world colonies, but these

Left: In the film's climactic moments, Deckard (Harrison Ford) scrambles for purchase on the edge of a building as he pursues Roy Batty (Rutger Hauer) across the rooftops.

four have come to Earth and must be hunted down and "retired"—or executed, as it looks to the casual observer. But are the replicants really inhuman? Or has humanity lost its way? Deckard must also figure out how Sean Young's Rachael fits in, the replicant who has no idea she is a replicant, and battle his own growing feelings for her.

That's only the tip of the iceberg of unanswered questions here. We don't know what devastated the environment and killed almost all life on Earth; we don't know why someone made the replicants so hard to find when they are also so hard to control (there's no other way of keeping track beyond a reaction assessment called the Voigt-Kampff test). And if empathy is the defining feature of humanity, according to the test, how come the humans can show so little empathy for their creations? Could any human in this reality pass the Voigt-Kampff, or is the purported villain, Rutger Hauer's Roy Batty, the film's true hero? It's Batty who has the most tragic narrative arc. He's stronger and smarter than the humans who created him; he has seen the wonders of the universe, fallen in love, and fought for his right to exist. But he is under a death sentence—and is all too aware of that fact. "All those moments will be lost in time, like tears in the rain," he mourns. "Time to die."

Such philosophical meatiness has kept the movie's cult growing for four decades now, wiping out the memory of its box-office underperformance and initially mixed reviews. Scott has gone back and tinkered with the film more than once before settling on the "final cut," removing the studio-mandated narration and unambiguously happy ending and added back much of the violence cut from the U.S. release. Notably, however, he and his leading man have never agreed on fundamental questions about the movie's (anti)hero: is Deckard himself a replicant? Scott's reinsertion of Deckard's dream of unicorns suggests that he might be; Ford has always remained adamant that he is not. Viewers can make up their own mind and debate their conclusions endlessly, and so contribute to the movie's legend.

Blade Runner has none of the easy charm of a *Star Wars* or its ilk; there are moments of levity but no real humor and hardly any sunlight. But it packs a

punch, in the end, as Batty chooses heroism over futile struggle and Deckard realizes the weight of his mistakes. On that rooftop, in the rain, we may not know what C-beams are or where to find the Tannhauser Gate, but we wish we did, and we are forced to consider our definition of humanity.

Above: Rachael (Sean Young) is a replicant who doesn't know she's a replicant. In the Philip K. Dick novel on which the film is based, it's made explicit that she is physically and emotionally modeled as an exact copy of Tyrell's (Joe Turkell) dead niece.

FACTS

ORIGINAL RELEASE DATE: June 25, 1982 (U.S.); September 9, 1982 (UK)
RUN TIME: 112 minutes

DID YOU KNOW?
- The movie was based on Philip K. Dick's story *Do Androids Dream of Electric Sheep?*—but the word "android" wasn't used, because it sounded too comical on-screen. Replication is a term used in cloning and sounded equally futuristic but less goofy.

FURTHER VIEWING
- *Brazil* (1985)
  Terry Gilliam's sci-fi classic is a weirder, zanier movie than *Blade Runner*, but it shares the same dark vision of a consumerist future, this one full of overwhelming bureaucracy and weird machines.

STAR TREK II: THE WRATH OF KHAN

1982

STAR TREK: THE MOTION PICTURE, RELEASED IN 1979, WAS SOMEWHAT OF A DISASTER.

As we join the crew of the USS *Enterprise*, they're tutoring a new generation of Starfleet recruits under now-Captain Spock (Leonard Nimoy). Now-Admiral James T. Kirk (William Shatner) is struggling with aging and chafing against the restrictions of his exalted rank. But they will soon be called back into action. While searching for a planet to test an experimental new device, the Genesis machine, Commander Pavel Chekov (Walter Koenig) stumbles across an old enemy of Kirk's, the genetically engineered Khan Noonien Singh (Ricardo Montalbán). Khan captures Chekov and his ship and sets out to exact revenge on Kirk, setting in motion one of cinema's great face-offs. The two never share a scene, but their mutual antipathy reaches across the void anyway.

The stroke of genius here was to focus on character, with a script that left a lot of room for Kirk, Spock (Leonard Nimoy), and Bones (DeForrest Kelley) to just hang out. It's also a movie that emphasizes the cleverness required to survive deep space. The thing about *Trek* that casual viewers often overlook is that the *Enterprise*'s survival usually came down to Captain Kirk out-thinking his opponents, not just out-punching them. It was a show that tackled big sci-fi concepts about life, the universe, and everything in among the green-skinned dancing girls—and in the big-ideas field, *Wrath of Khan* stands tall. This story discusses questions of regret and revenge, of self-sacrifice and aging, and of courage in the face of certain death (death is, after all, certain for everyone). But it does so with great

Left: Ricardo Montalbán had first played Khan Noonien Singh in the 1967 Star Trek episode "Space Seed," and returned 15 years later to reprise his role as the ultimate *Trek* baddie.

It has intriguing ideas and had a big budget, but it never captured the look or feel of the television series on which it was based. Amid skeptical reviews, it clawed back just enough money to get a green light on a less-expensive sequel. That follow-up, *Star Trek: The Wrath of Khan*, remains the best film in the *Star Trek* canon, and it is one of the best science-fiction adventures of the 1980s. Perhaps we owe *The Motion Picture* a vote of thanks after all.

gusto and a lust for life, taking in *Paradise Lost* and *Moby-Dick* and glorious 1980s mullets. There are moments of horror, and mystery, and what is, with 1990's *The Hunt for Red October* and 2003's *Master and Commander: The Far Side of the World*, one of cinema's most thrilling depictions of naval warfare. The nebula battle in the movie's last act is straight out of *Hornblower*, and the crippled ship's relative slowness only raises the tension as Kirk and Khan stalk one another through space. Montalbán's monomaniacal focus on Kirk's destruction takes the drama up another gear without quite falling into caricature; it's always clear that Khan sees himself as the wronged hero out for justice.

Director Nicholas Meyer (who also directed the second-best *Trek* movie, 1991's *The Undiscovered Country*) instinctively understood that the shining goodness of the *Enterprise* crew was best tested by a full-blown Shakespearean villain, someone with a flair for drama and meaty motives as big as the Federation's ideals. James Horner matched him with a theme-driven score that used only tiny moments of Alexander Courage's original music, relying instead on endlessly blendable mini themes for its leading men and for the *Enterprise* itself. His score is one of the decade's best.

Then there is the movie's superlative emotional climax, the death of Spock. It may have been born from Nimoy's reluctance to return without some dramatic send-off, but it became the film's greatest moment. From Spock's too-calm departure from the bridge to the somber note in Bones's voice as he asks Kirk to come down, there is not a false note in the setup. Kirk races to the radiation-flooded compartment, where Spock, swaying, faces his end, and the two get to share just a few words, most harking back to earlier conversations in the film, before Spock succumbs to his injuries. It is only then that Kirk seems to realize that their mutual devotion was the relationship that compensates him for all the regrets he struggled with earlier in the film. He did have a family, although perhaps not the one he envisioned. And it's that relationship that is the difference between Kirk and Khan. Kirk has an equal to rein in his worst instincts and point to his better

self; Spock is his guiding star. The franchise may have given in to the temptation to bring Spock back, in 1984's *The Search for Spock*, but the emotional whammy of this movie has never faded.

FACTS

ORIGINAL RELEASE DATE: June 4, 1982 (U.S.)
RUN TIME: 112 minutes

DID YOU KNOW?

- *The Wrath of Khan* features one of the first uses of computer-generated images on the big screen, with a then-groundbreaking 3-D landscape in the "Genesis effect" sequence.

FURTHER VIEWING

- *Star Trek IV: The Voyage Home* (1986) Skip *The Search for Spock*, which is okay but plot heavy, and race straight ahead to the crowd-pleasing antics of this time-traveling caper, wherein the crew of the *Enterprise* save the whales and the planet by venturing back to the mysterious world of the 1980s.

Below: The crew of the *Enterprise* (from left to right): Terrell (Paul Winfield), McCoy (DeForrest Kelley), Saavik (Kirstie Alley), Chekov (Walter Koenig), and Kirk (William Shatner).

TOOTSIE

1982

THE CROSS-DRESSING COMEDY HAS A LONG AND STORIED HISTORY, INCLUDING CLASSICS SUCH AS *BRINGING UP BABY*, *SOME LIKE IT HOT*, AND THE MULTIPLE-OSCAR NOMINEE *TOOTSIE*.

Their stories usually concern a man given entry to a woman's world under false pretenses, and they throw in a (straight) love story to shore up the leading man's masculinity. In the 2010s, the genre is beginning to fall out of favor, thanks to the efforts of transgender advocates and generally more open attitudes, so it's strange to go back and watch *Tootsie*, a smart and funny comedy about a straight man learning the error of his ways by acting as a woman. The good news is that Sydney Pollack's movie makes an effort to say something meaningful about gender, even if it doesn't always succeed.

We open on actor Michael Dorsey (Dustin Hoffman) meticulously preparing for a performance. From the acting class he teaches and the disastrous auditions he goes to ("I can be taller!"), it's clear this guy is passionate about his profession, although he works as a waiter to make ends meet until he gets that big break. On the same day that his student Sandy (Teri Garr) loses out on a role in the soap opera *Southwest General*, he learns that he won't be starring in a serious Broadway show. Michael's agent George (the director, Sydney Pollack) finally admits that no one will hire him because of his reputation as a perfectionist, and the actor decides to prove everyone wrong by landing the role that Sandy couldn't, hospital administrator Emily Kimberley, and by funding his roommate Jeff's (Bill Murray) play for himself to star in.

Posing as actress Dorothy Michaels, Michael is an immediate sensation. As Emily, he stands up to the leering Dr. Brewster/actor John Van Horn (George Gaynes), keeps the shooting schedule moving with improv, and becomes a fan favorite. Complicating matters, Michael sleeps with Sandy but forms a

Left: *Tootsie* isn't without some problematic elements, but it does explore some occasionally insightful points regarding gender.

searing crush on his gorgeous, insecure costar Julie (Jessica Lange, the movie's only Oscar winner). Dorothy becomes Julie's best friend, but Michael can't admit who he really is without losing her trust. "Don't you find being a woman in the eighties complicated?" asks Julie, and Dorothy agrees, although her complications are all self-inflicted.

It's astonishing now to see the levels of casual sexual harassment on the soap. Van Horn makes a point of kissing every female cast member and the director Rod (Dabney Coleman) is having an affair with two actresses while addressing all the women on set as "honey" or "tootsie." Even Dorsey, out of drag, has a pickup technique that's more than a little creepy. It takes being transformed into a woman for him to realize that women might also be people.

The movie's premise—a man has trouble finding work until he masquerades as a woman—is counter to general experience, because women statistically struggle to get the same opportunities as men. And unwisely Michael even tries to speak for women: "I've been an unemployed actor for twenty years, George! I know what it's like to just sit by the phone waiting for it to ring, and then when I finally get a job, I have absolutely no control; everyone else has the power and I have zip." At the same time, he keeps Sandy hanging by the phone. Pollack's movie quietly shows this hypocrisy, undermining Michael's claim that he's better at being a woman than women are.

Hoffman claimed that he never saw the movie as a comedy (suggesting that the actor shares some of his character's seriousness), but it's hard to see how he missed it. Dorothy's packed love life sees her negotiate passes from Julie's old-fashioned dad (the great Charles Durning) and Van Horn, while making passes at Julie as both Michael and Dorothy. It's a tangled web, and every time it comes close to crumbling down, there are hilarious scenes, such as when Van Horn assures Jeff that "nothing happened" with Dorothy, assuming that he's her husband. Eventually, Michael tries to concoct an appropriately far-fetched soap opera departure for Dorothy, revealing himself as her character's "brother" Edward Kimberley. Compared to many soap plots, this seems positively plausible, although

Emily's devoted fans must have felt betrayed by his destruction of their heroine.

Still, *Tootsie* goes farther than other movies of its kind in grappling with the question of what we can learn from one another's experience. Living as a woman teaches Michael the empathy to be a better man, making him more restrained and polite in his dealings with others. But it's not until he gives up the masquerade that he can finally become the best version of himself. Dorothy changed him more than he could have guessed.

FACTS

ORIGINAL RELEASE DATE:
December 17, 1982 (U.S.); April 28, 1983 (UK)
RUN TIME: 111 minutes

DID YOU KNOW?
- This was Geena Davis's big-screen debut; she plays actress April, Dorothy's uninhibited dressing-room companion.

FURTHER VIEWING
- *Yentl* (1983)
  Barbra Streisand's Golden Globe–winning directorial debut reverses the *Tootsie* dynamic, with a Jewish girl in 1904 Poland pretending to be a boy in order to be allowed to take Talmudic study. It's more serious than *Tootsie*, and has even better tunes.

THE THING

1982

TWO MOVIES ABOUT ALIENS OPENED IN THE SUMMER OF 1982. ONE OF THEM WAS *E.T. THE EXTRA-TERRESTRIAL*, WHICH TAUGHT US THAT ALIENS WERE JUST FRIENDS WE HADN'T MET YET.

John Carpenter's *The Thing*, the other, was less optimistic, scorned by critics, and largely ignored by the public, making just $19.6 million on a $15 million budget in the U.S. Not a flop, but also nowhere near a hit. But the years have been kind to this Antarctic horror, and repeat viewing has burnished its reputation to something close to Spielberg's masterpiece.

In some ways, it's a classic haunted-house movie with just a thin veneer of science fiction. An American Antarctic survey team, out on the ice, see a Norwegian helicopter crew apparently chasing an innocent malamute across the wasteland. The chopper crashes, killing all aboard, and the kind-hearted Yanks bring the dog back to their base. Big mistake.

The injured mutt dies, but that is not the end of its story. The body turns inside out and disgorges something horrible, an alien that was frozen in

Above: Kurt Russell plays R. J. MacReady, Antarctic helicopter pilot and one of the quintessential John Carpenter leading men. Russell helped Carpenter develop his ideas for the film, but was the final principal actor to formally sign on.

the ice for millennia before it was uncovered by the Norwegians. This shape-shifting monstrosity starts picking its way through the station team, mimicking its victims and leaving blood, guts, and all-encompassing paranoia in its wake. Who is still human and who is an alien impostor? How can any of the team trust one another?

The weather outside is not survivable and there is no help to be called, or their rescuers will also get infected. So the close-knit team is trapped in close quarters with something they cannot fathom. They're also quickly traumatized by the horror of the Thing ("Mac wants the flamethrower!"). Thanks to Rob Bottin's enduringly grotesque effects, something he labored over every single day for a year (he even slept in his workshop on a regular basis), they see a tentacled nightmare dog, friends turned inside out, and the single worst chest defibrillation ever as a Thing-victim's chest opens up and bites off a doctor's hands. Oh, and then the victim's head detaches itself and goes for a walk. It's outrageous and gruesome and impossible to forget.

This is, in other words, John Carpenter not pulling his punches. As a fan of the Howard Hawks– produced *The Thing from Another World*, taken from the same source novella as this, Carpenter had been reluctant to take on this project, but when he finally did engage, he pressed for more effects and location work to push the story to the limit. And despite tinkering with some conventional endings, he went with something fresh. Unlike the original novella, John W. Campbell Jr.'s *Who Goes There?*, there is no happy ending, and even the note of unease in that original movie adaptation pales in comparison to this nihilistic finale. It comes down to two survivors, our hero R. J. MacReady (Kurt Russell at his most charismatic) and Childs (Keith David), in a kind of Mexican standoff. The two are outside in the cold, minutes from freezing to death, and unsure if they can trust one another to be Thing-free. So they just sit, and drink, and wait for the cold to take them.

The Thing has been a major influence ever since; Quentin Tarantino said of it, "The paranoia amongst the characters was so strong, trapped in that enclosure for so long, that it just bounced off all

ORIGINAL RELEASE DATE: June 25, 1982 (U.S.); August 26, 1982 (UK)
RUN TIME: 106 minutes

DID YOU KNOW?

- Several foodstuffs were used for the creature effects, including mayonnaise, jelly, creamed corn, and microwaved bubble gum.

FURTHER VIEWING

- *The Fly* (1986)
  David Cronenberg also tackles a '50s sci-fi classic with gory, disturbing results, turning Jeff Goldblum gradually into the tragi-horrifying Brundlefly.

FACTS

the walls until it had nowhere to go but out into the audience. That is what I was trying to achieve with *The Hateful Eight*." There's even a poster for it hanging up in Netflix's *Stranger Things*. And it's endured because we will always fear the unknown, and the elements, and each other. Worryingly, the movie may have been onto something with its monster in the ice. Arctic survey teams have uncovered ancient viruses beneath the thawing permafrost, and a Russian boy died after contracting anthrax from an old outbreak that had been frozen over. One scientist even injected himself with thawed-out, 3.5-million-year-old bacteria, just to see what would happen (to date, he has not mutated into anything). Climate change has at least spared us alien shape-shifters so far. But "Man is the warmest place to hide" said the tagline for *The Thing*, and who knows what else is lurking under the ice? *The Thing* may yet prove prescient. But for now, it's simply one of the most tense, most thrilling horrors ever made.

Below: The film's tagline and poster became one of the most famous of the 1980s, though Drew Struzan's art has little to do with the story.

The ultimate in alien terror.

THE THING

1983 HIGHLIGHTS

Star Wars ruled the box office for the third time, but the family drama *Terms of Endearment* dominated the Oscars. Comedians like Eddie Murphy and Michael Keaton started making inroads at the box office, while a young star named Tom Cruise proved a force to be reckoned with...

HIGHEST-GROSSING FILMS (U.S.)

1. *Return of the Jedi*	20th Century Fox	$252,583,617
2. *Terms of Endearment*	Paramount	$108,423,489
3. *Flashdance*	Paramount	$92,921,203
4. *Trading Places*	Paramount	$90,404,800
5. *WarGames*	United Artists	$79,567,667
6. *Octopussy*	United Artists	$67,800,000
7. *Sudden Impact*	Warner Bros.	$67,642,693
8. *Staying Alive*	Paramount	$64,892,670
9. *Mr. Mom*	20th Century Fox	$64,783,827
10. *Risky Business*	Warner Bros.	$63,541,777

AT THE GOLDEN GLOBES

Best Picture (Drama)	*Terms of Endearment*
Best Picture (Comedy/Musical)	*Yentl*
Best Director	Barbra Streisand, *Yentl*
Best Actor (Drama)	Robert Duvall, *Tender Mercies*;
	Tom Courtenay, *The Dresser* (tie)
Best Actor (Comedy/Musical)	Michael Caine, *Educating Rita*
Best Actress (Drama)	Shirley MacLaine, *Terms of Endearment*
Best Actress (Comedy/Musical)	Julie Walters, *Educating Rita*

CANNES FILM FESTIVAL

Palme d'Or winner

The Ballad of Narayama,
Shohei Imamura

NOTABLE DEATHS

George Cukor, January 24	Director, *The Philadelphia Story* and *The Women*
Gloria Swanson, April 4	Actor, *Sunset Blvd* and *Indiscreet*
Dolores Del Rio, April 11	Actor, *The Abandoned* and *Flying Down to Rio*
Norma Shearer, June 12	Actor, *The Women* and *The Divorcee*
David Niven, July 29	Actor, *Casino Royale* and *Murder by Death*
Luis Bunuel, July 29	Director, *Belle du Jour* and *The Discreet Charm of the Bourgeoise*

AT THE OSCARS

Best Picture	*Terms of Endearment*
Best Director	James L. Brooks, *Terms of Endearment*
Best Actor	Robert Duvall, *Tender Mercies*
Best Actress	Shirley MacLaine, *Terms of Endearment*

THIS YEAR'S BIG OSCARS INJUSTICE

Martin Scorsese's generally underrated *The King of Comedy* didn't even get a nomination for Best Picture, but it has aged more gracefully than the totally fine *Terms of Endearment*.

FUTURE MOVIE STAR BIRTHS

February 23: Emily Blunt, *The Devil Wears Prada* and *A Quiet Place*

March 1: Lupita Nyong'o, *12 Years a Slave* and *Black Panther*

August 4: Greta Gerwig, *Mistress America* and *Lady Bird*

August 11: Chris Hemsworth, *Thor* and *Ghostbusters*

October 3: Tessa Thompson, *Thor: Ragnarok* and *Creed*

NOTABLE FILM DEBUTS

Jim Carrey, *All in Good Taste*

John Cusack, *Class*

Andy Garcia, *Blue Skies Again*

Nicole Kidman, *Bush Christmas*

Kiefer Sutherland, *Max Dugan Returns*

THE EVIL DEAD & EVIL DEAD II

1983 1987

THROUGHOUT THE 1980S, THERE WERE REGULAR OUTBREAKS OF MORAL PANIC IN THE UNITED STATES AND THE UNITED KINGDOM ABOUT "VIDEO NASTIES" AND WHAT KIDS MIGHT BE WATCHING.

Chief among the targets were spectacular horrors, such as Sam Raimi's *The Evil Dead* and *Evil Dead II*, movies that went so far into grotesque terror that they come back out the other side into comedy. The Moral Majority still panicked, of course, but they looked silly, because audiences loved these movies as much for their absurdity as for their gross-out scares.

The Evil Dead began when Raimi was shooting a tense scene in his first movie, *It's Murder*, and got to thinking that it might be interesting to try horror. He researched what worked in local drive-ins, shot a short version of the film he planned called *Within the Woods*, and used that to spark investor interest in a feature-length version of what came to be called *The Evil Dead*.

It's a simple story. Five college friends head to a remote cabin in the woods for a getaway. A few ominous signs should probably give them pause: a steering wheel that twists suddenly, almost crashing the car; locals waving a warning; a bridge that almost collapses under them—but they continue on, oblivious. At the cabin, they discover a recording left by a history professor who taped his translation of a strange old book, the *Necronomicon*. When they play the tape, invisible and demonic forces start to carry out gory attacks on the gang. There is a still-shocking scene of a tree's branches raping one victim and the drawn-out pencil-stabbing of another in the leg. With each injury the victim becomes possessed in turn, and the horror amps up another gear. These "deadites" possess four of the five students and,

Left: Bruce Campbell equipped to battle deadites in his first outing as cult icon Ash Williams.

when the cursed book (the *Necronomicon*) that brought them to life is burned, they dissolve horribly into Technicolor goo. Only Bruce Campbell's Ash survives the night.

The Evil Dead was a success, unlike Raimi's next movie (*Crimewave*), so he returned to the world for another pass. A few years after the original, 1986's *Evil Dead II* tells almost the same story but is technically a sequel: the scenes of Ash and his recast girlfriend Linda (now Denise Bixler) at the beginning are intended as a flashback. However, this time Linda returns as a deadite and Ash semi-accidentally beheads her with a shovel, before himself becoming possessed until dawn chases the infection away. But after the history professor's two kids and their two redneck guides arrive as bonus victims, the movie plays the same story on a bigger effects budget. There's another girl attacked by trees (although less graphically), another monster trapped in the cellar, and another curse to be undone. With almost ten times as much money at his disposal, Raimi relies less on (cheap) camera angles and quick cuts and more on stop-motion monsters and spectacular moments, such as Ash's self-dismemberment, when he cuts off his own possessed arm.

The original movie had wildly inventive effects, deliberate comedy elements, and a Charleston ditty over its credits to underline its non-seriousness. But most of the things we remember about the two movies—the chainsaw arm, "Groovy baby"—come from the second one, which goes so much farther over the top that it's clearly a horror-comedy. Linda's severed head and semi-skeletal body do a stop-motion dance in the finest tradition of legendary animator Ray Harryhausen. A corpse's eyeball, dislodged by Ash's blow, flies into a girl's mouth. The makeup is more grotesque, the effects even more elaborate, and the body count higher. And then a giant tree monster caps things off and Ash is sucked into a time vortex to AD 1300, setting up 1992's medieval *Army of Darkness*.

The Evil Dead and its successor were hugely influential, not least because Raimi's decision to shoot a short film as a trailer was mimicked by Ethan Coen (assistant editor on *Evil Dead*) and his brother Joel for

ORIGINAL RELEASE DATE:
The Evil Dead, April 15, 1983 (U.S.); January 16, 1983 (UK)
Evil Dead II, March 13, 1987 (U.S.); June 26, 1987 (UK)
RUN TIME: 142 minutes

DID YOU KNOW?

- The yellow car from the first *Evil Dead*, a 1973 Oldsmobile Delta 88 Royale, appears in almost all of Sam Raimi's movies. He even disassembled it and hid parts in his Western movie *The Quick and the Dead* and his fantasy film *Oz the Great and Powerful*.

FURTHER VIEWING

- *An American Werewolf in London* (1981)
  John Landis's horror-comedy about a tourist bitten by a werewolf shares *Evil Dead*'s commitment to impressive, gnarly effects, although with a much higher budget and proper location shooting around London.

FACTS

the first film of their Oscar-winning career. Raimi's gonzo approach to horror, effective editing, and those swooping point-of-view shots of the monster are still used everywhere today. The director himself paid tribute to his roots even on big movies such as *Spider-Man 2*. *The Evil Dead* was directly homaged in Drew Goddard's *The Cabin in the Woods*, remade in 2013 (one of the few 1980s movies redone well), and subverted in *Tucker & Dale vs. Evil*. It influenced Edgar Wright (*Shaun of the Dead*) and *Lord of the Rings* director Peter Jackson's early work (movies such as *Bad Taste* and *Dead Alive*). It's also a blast to watch, if you can stomach the gore. Groovy.

Left: The quintessential horror zombie-arm-from-a-grave shot used on promo posters and VHS jackets.

1984 HIGHLIGHTS

Look at the top ten films for 1984, and you'll see a recognizably modern list of fantasy and sci-fi blockbusters; all that's missing is a couple of superheroes. This was a huge year for geek cinema, with *Ghostbusters* and *Gremlins* standing alongside Indiana Jones's second outing.

HIGHEST-GROSSING FILMS (U.S.)

1. *Beverly Hills Cop*	Paramount	$234,760,478
2. *Ghostbusters*	Columbia	$229,242,989
3. *Indiana Jones and the Temple of Doom*	Paramount	$179,870,271
4. *Gremlins*	Warner Bros.	$153,083,102
5. *The Karate Kid*	Columbia	$90,815,558
6. *Police Academy*	Warner Bros.	$81,198,894
7. *Footloose*	Paramount	$80,035,402
8. *Romancing the Stone*	20th Century Fox	$76,572,238
9. *Star Trek III: The Search for Spock*	Paramount	$76,471,076
10. *Splash*	Touchstone Pictures	$69,821,334

AT THE GOLDEN GLOBES

Best Picture (Drama)	*Amadeus*
Best Picture (Comedy/Musical)	*Romancing the Stone*
Best Director	Milos Forman, *Amadeus*
Best Actor (Drama)	F. Murray Abraham, *Amadeus*
Best Actor (Comedy/Musical)	Dudley Moore, *Micki & Maude*
Best Actress (Drama)	Sally Field, *Places in the Heart*
Best Actress (Comedy/Musical)	Kathleen Turner, *Romancing the Stone*

CANNES FILM FESTIVAL

Palme d'Or winner
Paris, Texas,
Wim Wenders

NOTABLE DEATHS

Ethel Merman, February 15	Actor and singer, *It's a Mad Mad Mad Mad World* and *Airplane!*
James Mason, July 27	Actor, *North by Northwest* and *A Star Is Born*
Richard Burton, August 5	Actor, *Who's Afraid of Virginia Woolf?* and *1984*
Francois Truffaut, October 21	Director and actor, *The 400 Blows* and *Jules et Jim*
Sam Peckinpah, December 28	Director, *The Wild Bunch* and *Straw Dogs*

AT THE OSCARS

Best Picture	*Amadeus*
Best Director	Milos Forman, *Amadeus*
Best Actor	F. Murray Abraham, *Amadeus*
Best Actress	Sally Field, *Places in the Heart*

THIS YEAR'S BIG OSCARS INJUSTICE

The real outrage is Stevie Wonder's schmaltzy *I Just Called to Say I Love You* winning Best Original Song over *Ghostbusters*, *Footloose*, and *Against All Odds*.

FUTURE MOVIE STAR BIRTHS

April 10: Mandy Moore, *Tangled* and *47 Meters Down*

April 18: America Ferrera, *Real Women Have Curves* and *Ugly Betty*

June 19: Paul Dano, *There Will Be Blood* and *Little Miss Sunshine*

September 3: Garrett Hedlund, *Mudbound* and *Tron: Legacy*

November 22: Scarlett Johansson, *Avengers* and *Lost in Translation*

NOTABLE FILM DEBUTS

Jennifer Connelly, *Once Upon a Time in America*

Johnny Depp, *A Nightmare on Elm Street*

Val Kilmer, *Top Secret!*

Frances McDormand, *Blood Simple*

Ken Watanabe, *MacArthur's Children*

Michelle Yeoh, *The Owl vs. Bombo*

THE TERMINATOR

JAMES CAMERON CLAIMS THAT THE IDEA FOR HIS BREAKTHROUGH MOVIE CAME TO HIM IN A DREAM, BUT IT'S THE LOGIC OF NIGHTMARES THAT DRIVES THIS TIME-TRAVEL HORROR.

Left: Stan Winston's prosthetics work for *The Terminator* included the creation of a fake Arnold Schwarzenegger head with robotic segments.

Below: A posed publicity still of the T-800 (Arnold Schwarzenegger), looking markedly more human than he does in the movie.

"They can't be bargained with. It can't be reasoned with. It doesn't feel remorse or pity or fear. And it absolutely will not stop, ever, until you are dead." This could describe any classic monster. And unlike its sequels, this one is as much horror as action, with its singular, overwhelming monster, girlish victim, and pulsating narrative drive.

After a precredit glimpse of a future dystopia to let us know there is a science-fiction theme, honest, we're taken straight into a typical Friday for poodle-haired Sarah Connor (Linda Hamilton), a terrible waitress and fluffy young woman who seems like she'd be unable to protect herself against a housefly. She's the kind of girl who wears a frumpy peach cardigan to go on a date, which is bad even accounting for 1980s fashion. Still, perhaps her pet iguana suggests that she has unconventional interests hidden underneath, and the potential for greater things.

But late one night, a naked form appears in a ball of lightning up by the Griffith Observatory. It is the mesomorphic Arnold Schwarzenegger, fresh from his bodybuilding career and easing into acting by way of a quick stop to relieve some unfortunate punks (including future Cameron regular Bill Paxton) of their clothes, boots, motorcycle, and lives. He is playing the titular killer, Cyberdyne Systems model T-800, an unstoppable killing machine wrapped in a thin veneer of human flesh.

Across town, the shivering Kyle Reese (Michael Biehn) lands in a similar light show, but this newcomer is skinny and desperate and immediately hounded by the law. While Arnie's Terminator begins his quest to eliminate every Sarah Connor in the phone book, Reese is a cowering, creepy-looking fugitive stalking our Sarah for reasons that are, initially, unclear. It's an unsettling beginning, but even if you follow the Hollywood version of Occam's razor (always trust the more handsome guy), it's clear that something is deeply wrong.

While Brad Fiedel's score pulses like a panicked heartbeat, the impasse comes to a head. The Terminator makes his first attempt on Sarah's life, Reese rescues her ("Come with me if you want to live"), and we're off. Kyle followed the Terminator back from the future to save Sarah, because she is destined to become the mother of the man who will save humanity in a war against the machines. Reese chronicles the war of the future, the kind of dystopian wasteland so horrific that humans have no choice but to grow mullets in order to survive.

Reese teaches her how to fight back, tutors her in the rules of Terminator resistance, and keeps her alive long enough for the two to get it on. After all, "I came across time for you, Sarah" is one of the all-time greatest chat-up lines. It's a small part of the narrative, but it lands—*Terminator* is one of the better romances of the 1980s. Kyle's absolute belief in Sarah's toughness visibly adds steel to her spine; soon she's hauling him around despite his injuries and delivering a kiss-off line ("You're terminated!") that makes up for in attitude what it lacks in wordplay.

As the Terminator closes in and the action ramps up through a high-speed chase, Cameron proves himself as a director in a killer last act with a great fake-out. "We did it, Kyle, we got it," sobs Sarah Connor on her lover's shoulder—but behind them a pile of truck wreckage falls apart as a robot skeleton emerges (some of Stan Winston's finest work). Reese blows the thing up and still half its torso grasps after its target, before the two take refuge in the nearest building, a factory, for a final showdown. There, we get the neat metaphor of a robotic, automated production

sequence proving the Terminator's undoing as it is finally crushed. It's as if the Terminator goes back in time to be killed by his grandfather. Kind of. It's *Back to the Future: The Machine Years*—or would be, until *T2* rewrote the script and endless sequels kept tinkering with that ending.

But the original is a classic for a reason. From Arnie's controlled, implacable pursuit of Connor ("I'll be back") to Reese's desperate heroism, there's barely a dud note. And it ends on a moment of ominous optimism, as a tougher and visibly pregnant Sarah Connor drives into a wide-open future. She'll be back.

ORIGINAL RELEASE DATE: October 26, 1984 (U.S.); January 11, 1985 (UK)
RUN TIME: 106 minutes

DID YOU KNOW?

* *The Terminator*'s budget was just $6.5 million. Seven years later, *Terminator 2: Judgment Day* would become the most expensive movie ever made when it cost $100 million.

FURTHER VIEWING

* *The Abyss* (1989)
  James Cameron began his deep-sea obsession with this 1989 adventure, which morphs from disaster movie into sci-fi epic.

FACTS

"I'LL BE BACK."

The Terminator (Arnold Schwarzenegger), *THE TERMINATOR*

GHOSTBUSTERS

1984

THE STORY GOES THAT HALFWAY THROUGH LUNCH DURING THE MAKING OF *GHOSTBUSTERS*, DIRECTOR IVAN REITMAN AND HIS CAST WERE WORRYING ABOUT THE BUDGET, THE EFFECTS, AND HOW THEY COULD POSSIBLY MAKE THIS STRANGE SUPERNATURAL COMEDY WORK.

Amid all these anxieties, Bill Murray laughed, turned to Dan Aykroyd, and said, "Pal, you've just written one of the biggest comedies of all time. Relax." In this, as in so many other things in life, Bill Murray was entirely correct. *Ghostbusters* was a critical and commercial triumph, the standard by which all other effects comedies are still judged.

It had originally been written by Aykroyd in the early 1980s for himself and John Belushi as a future-set, time-traveling horror about two guys featuring evil ghosts. Aykroyd has a lifelong interest in the supernatural, but he lost heart in the idea after Belushi's early death and threw it in a drawer. Still, he could never entirely let it lie. Eventually, he showed it to Reitman, and the director saw intriguing possibilities in the concept. He liked the blue-collar sensibility of regular guys doggedly fighting ghosts, but he pushed for a contemporary Manhattan setting—not least because it would make the movie's budget something that a studio might actually be able to afford. Aykroyd went back to work, this time with Harold Ramis beside him, and *Ghostbusters* began to take shape.

What settled into place was the story of three, later four, guys who discover—in rapid succession—a way to detect, entrap, and hold ghosts. Egon (Ramis) is the conceptual genius, Ray (Aykroyd) the engineer, and Venkman (Murray) the scientist-salesman who manages their enthusiasm and keeps it pointed in a vaguely profitable direction. Having lost their Columbia University positions over their madcap supernatural theories, they try to turn haunting into profit by offering their services as spirit exterminators or, if you will, Ghostbusters.

Their first few jobs are borderline disastrous, resulting in more property damage than any poltergeist could dream of, but things change when Venkman takes a call from Dana Barrett (Sigourney Weaver). She has a hard-to-pin-down haunting, which is good news for Venkman, because he formed an immediate crush and wants an excuse to keep visiting. He's in luck, kind of: the small, initial signs—televisions turning on for no reason, eggs jumping from their carton and cooking spontaneously, and

Below: Ray (Dan Aykroyd) and Winston (Ernie Hudson) step out of ECTO-1 to confront the latest spectral menace.

corporate logo. The movie is scary at times but never *too* scary; "He slimed me" is as horrific as it gets for most of the running time.

And the script is, hands down, Aykroyd's best, with even throwaway lines offering glorious results, such as "You forget I was present at an undersea, unexplained mass sponge migration" or "Listen! Do you smell something?" His enthusiasm is balanced beautifully by Murray's bottomless cynicism ("No job is too big, no fee is too big.") and Ramis's deadpan nerdishness ("I'm always serious"; his hobby is collecting "spores, molds, and fungus"), in a dynamic that never gets old.

As Murray predicted, the movie broke box office records, selling more than sixty-eight million tickets in its initial U.S. run and becoming a cultural touchstone all over the world. This was partly due to the Oscar-nominated theme song by Ray Parker Jr., and to Michael C. Gross's iconic *Ghostbusters* logo poster. Kids loved the proton packs, the slime, and ran around quoting lines such as "Who you gonna call?" But most of all, the huge success was due to the movie's glorious, giddy laughs. To misquote the theme, busting (with laughter) still makes us feel good.

nightmare portals to another dimension in the refrigerator—are signs of much worse to come. Dana's building is at the center of some terrifying supernatural activity that signals the return of an old, dangerous, apocalyptic god-ghost called Gozer and its herald Zuul (Slavitza Jovan). The Ghostbusters, now four with the arrival of Ernie Hudson's sensible but underserved Winston Zeddemore, must take down a marshmallow man the size of a building in order to keep the city safe.

Ghostbusters' influence is visible in so many movies made since 1984, in that hugely ramped-up last act, the fast-talking wit of its leads, and its clueless scientist characters. But few imitators can rival its magic-in-a-bottle tone. The three leads were comedians who knew each other well and sparked off each other's energy like jazz musicians, aided by a supporting cast that included Hudson, Rick Moranis's gloriously dweeby Louis Tully, William Atherton's smarmy Walter Peck, and Weaver's steadying Dana. It also had inventive ghosts, from the grotesque green Slimer, to the still-disturbing library ghost, to that unlikely finale against a

Left: The original three Ghostbusters Venkman (Bill Murray), Ray (Aykroyd), and Egon (Harold Ramis) pose for the camera. They're ready to believe you!

FACTS

ORIGINAL RELEASE DATE: June 8, 1984 (U.S.); December 7, 1984 (UK)
RUN TIME: 103 minutes

DID YOU KNOW?

* The marshmallow that covers the street after the explosion of the marshmallow man was actually made of shaving foam.

FURTHER VIEWING

* *Ghostbusters 2* (1989)
  It has a poor reputation, but there are loads of funny moments in the belated sequel, with Peter MacNicol possessed by the malevolent spirit of Vigo the Carpathian and turned into an evil version of Mary Poppins.

BEST MOVIE THEME SONGS OF THE 1980S

The 1980s was a golden era for the movie theme song, the specially composed pop hit that would—ideally—play on a loop on MTV and every major radio station while your film was in theaters, creating a tidal wave of demand for the film itself. Some of them were bigger than the film that inspired them ("Nine to Five," "Against All Odds") and some are inseparable from it ("Ghostbusters"). Just try not to get these stuck in your head.

"GHOSTBUSTERS," RAY PARKER JR., *GHOSTBUSTERS*

"LET THE RIVER RUN," CARLY SIMON, *WORKING GIRL*

"THE POWER OF LOVE," HUEY LEWIS AND THE NEWS, *BACK TO THE FUTURE*

"WHAT A FEELING," *FLASHDANCE*

"9 TO 5," DOLLY PARTON, *NINE TO FIVE*

"AGAINST ALL ODDS (TAKE A LOOK AT ME NOW),"
PHIL COLLINS, *AGAINST ALL ODDS*

"FAME," IRENE CARA, *FAME*

"A KIND OF MAGIC," QUEEN, *HIGHLANDER*

"EYE OF THE TIGER," SURVIVOR, *ROCKY III*

HONORABLE MENTIONS

"(I've Had) The Time of My Life," Bill Medley and Jennifer Warner,
　　　Dirty Dancing
"Footloose," Kenny Loggins, *Footloose*
"Take My Breath Away," Berlin, *Top Gun*
"Purple Rain," Prince, *Purple Rain*
"Oh Yeah," Yello, *Ferris Bueller's Day Off*
"When the Goin' Gets Tough, the Tough Get Going," Billy Ocean,
　　　Romancing the Stone
"Nothing's Gonna Stop Us Now," Starship, *Mannequin*
"Up Where We Belong," Joe Cocker and Jennifer Warnes,
　　　An Officer and a Gentleman
"We Don't Need Another Hero," Tina Turner, *Mad Max
　　　Beyond Thunderdome*

GREMLINS

THE 1980S WAS A GREAT ERA FOR NONTRADITIONAL CHRISTMAS MOVIES.

We had action Christmases in *Die Hard* and *Lethal Weapon*, replacing Christmas lights with explosions and trees with terrorists. In *Scrooged*, we got a yuppie holiday complete with branded towels, and *A Christmas Story*'s nostalgic charm is built around a kid's deep desire for a gun. Yuletide even went full slasher in *Silent Night, Deadly Night*. But perhaps the most twisted of the lot is *Gremlins*, which sees the idyllic, snow-covered small town of Kingston Falls infested by cackling, lethal little monsters on Christmas Eve.

The story begins when wannabe inventor Randall Peltzer (Hoyt Axton) buys a fuzzy creature called Gizmo in a run-down Chinatown junk shop as a present for his son, Billy (Zach Galligan). It's not for sale, but the owner's grandson sells it anyway and makes sure to tell him the rules for its care: avoid bright lights, especially daylight; don't let it get wet; and never, ever, feed it after midnight. Inevitably, all three rules are broken, and the latter two cause a disastrous plague of chittering monsters.

Anyone frustrated by the logic of those rules can take comfort in the call that legendary science-fiction author Harlan Ellison made to screenwriter Chris Columbus shortly after the movie's release. "His biggest complaint," Columbus told *Empire* magazine, "was the fact that these creatures could be in the snow and essentially if they went inside they would get wet and multiply. And it's always midnight somewhere! But then it's meant as a joke."

Columbus was inspired to create the gremlins by a plague of mice in the drafty Manhattan loft apartment he lived in while trying to get his break (he would go on to direct the first two Harry Potter movies), and his original script had an even harder

edge to it. In the first incarnation, the gremlins rampaged through a McDonald's, eating the people but leaving the Big Macs untouched. While the finished movie sees Billy's mom (Frances Lee McCain) nuking one of the critters in her microwave, the original script had them behead her and roll her noggin down the stairs.

Still, Steven Spielberg picked it up, wearing his producer's hat, and offered it to Joe Dante. Spielberg and Dante had worked together on the anthology *Twilight Zone: The Movie*, and Spielberg liked Dante's

Above: Gizmo the Mogwai looking adorable in his original Chinatown home. Just don't expose him to bright light, get him wet, or feed him after midnight.

last feature, *The Howling*. Both thought Columbus's script could be made into a low-budget Christmas horror, but it gradually morphed into something less familiar, less obvious. Twenty rewrites later, *Gremlins* had become more of a comedy than a straight horror, and instead of a Christmas release it bagged a prestigious summer date in the United States (in fact, it went up directly against *Ghostbusters*).

Still, it's a weird comedy. The gremlins hide in Christmas trees to cause maximum havoc and take delight in chaos more than they do in killing. They're more often heard chittering and laughing but unseen, although that was more for practical reasons than dramatic choice. The gremlins were kept off-screen as much as possible because puppeteering them was a nightmare; the climactic scene, where hundreds take over a movie theater, involved scores of puppeteers, some of them wearing a gremlin on each hand and another as a hat. Gizmo caused even more problems. Spielberg had suggested keeping the fuzzy pet alive, but he was such a limited puppet and so hard to manipulate that the entire crew soon grew to hate him with a passion (the shot of Gizmo tied to a dartboard was a crew member's suggestion).

The human cast was easier to handle. Galligan is guileless and likable as Billy, the good guy who's technically (but not morally) responsible for the plague. Phoebe Cates is weird and inspired as his barmaid girlfriend Kate; her bizarre account of her father's death is the tragi-comic highlight of the movie, although *everyone* tried to persuade Dante to cut it, and it remained only when Spielberg backed him up. And so we learn that Kate hates Christmas because her father once dressed up as Santa Claus and broke his neck attempting to climb down the chimney. Kids, don't try it at home.

It's no accident that Kingston Falls closely resembles *It's a Wonderful Life*'s town of Bedford Falls. *Gremlins* deliberately takes all those small-town Christmas traditions and slashes them with its many tiny claws. But it's become a beloved classic in its turn. Perhaps, in the end, the true meaning of Christmas is surviving the destruction of your entire town at the hands of tiny malign fiends.

Right: Definitive proof that *Gremlins* is a Christmas film.

ORIGINAL RELEASE DATE: June 8, 1984 (U.S.); December 7, 1984 (UK)
RUN TIME: 106 minutes

DID YOU KNOW?
- Rejected ideas for a sequel included sending the gremlins to Las Vegas or Mars. In the end, Dante returned to make 1990's *Gremlins 2: The New Batch*, set in a New York skyscraper.

FURTHER VIEWING
- *Young Sherlock Holmes* (1985)
  Another Christopher Columbus–scripted, Spielberg-produced affair, this take on the iconic detective is a surprisingly grown-up affair, despite the title.

FACTS

BEVERLY HILLS COP

1984

EDDIE MURPHY WAS ONE OF THE BIGGEST STAND-UP STARS IN THE WORLD IN 1984, WITH HIS DELIRIOUS TV ROUTINE ALREADY A CLASSIC AND FOUR YEARS ON *SATURDAY NIGHT LIVE* BEHIND HIM.

He'd had a hit movie with his debut in *48 Hrs.*, opposite Nick Nolte, and followed that up with *Trading Places*, alongside fellow *SNL* graduate Dan Aykroyd. But it was 1984 when Murphy, still only twenty-three, took his first solo lead in the movie that confirmed him as a megastar. *Beverly Hills Cop* was the crucible that transformed every ounce of his charisma, a fair helping of his humor, and an unsuspected knack for action into box-office gold. Murphy went into the movie as a rising star; he emerged a confirmed A-lister. And yet it almost didn't happen.

The notion behind *Beverly Hills Cop*—in which a tough city cop visits the fanciest neighborhood in the country—had been kicking around Hollywood since the late 1970s. This was when Michael Eisner, the future head of Disney, had the idea after getting a speeding ticket. Or when Don Simpson, the maverick producer who would transform the action movie with his partner Jerry Bruckheimer, had it. Or possibly future studio founder Jeffrey Katzenberg. Success has a thousand fathers and the story's origin is disputed. In any case, the idea morphed into a straight action movie about a streetwise Pittsburgh detective named Elly Axel, with Mickey Rourke attached to star.

When rewrites pulled the movie toward comedy and Rourke left, possible replacements included James Caan and Al Pacino, but it was Sylvester Stallone who came closest. As befits the star of *Rocky* and *Rambo*, he took a pass at the script, amping up the violence so

far that he later compared his version to the opening scenes of *Saving Private Ryan*. But his ideas—including playing chicken in a Lamborghini with a villain in a train—were too expensive, and he left weeks before shooting was due to start. Enter Murphy, and another rewrite to suit his comic strengths, saving millions by emphasizing gags over gunfire.

The movie opens wittily, on an industrial Detroit landscape. The caption "Beverly Hills" appears, pausing for a moment so that you wonder if someone charged with the credits lost his or her mind, before "COP" is scrawled across the top. Time to meet Axel Foley (Eddie Murphy), the fast-talking Detroit cop who uses evidence from one bust to entrap another gang. His operation goes awry, putting him in the bad books with his boss, Inspector Todd (Gilbert R. Hill, once a real Detroit homicide detective). It becomes a problem when his childhood friend Mikey (James Russo), a petty criminal, is killed and Axel is barred from investigating. Obviously, that won't stop him, and he heads to Beverly Hills in search of those responsible.

Axel raises a ruckus at a swank hotel ("I am a reporter from *Rolling Stone* magazine in town to interview Michael Jackson!") until he's given a suite, and he sets to work. There's no doubt in his mind whodunnit, especially when he meets Steven Berkoff's laughably sinister Victor Maitland; however, proving it is the problem. Foley's path soon crosses with two genteel local cops, Sergeant Taggart (John Ashton) and Billy Rosewood (Judge Reinhold), who find themselves working with the Detroit detective and eventually corrupted by his maverick ways.

The movie is stuffed with great supporting characters, such as Bronson Pinchot's Serge, and conforms to the rule that no policeman in the 1980s could solve a case without visiting at least one strip club. But there are also scenes showing the police heavy-handedness that awaits anyone who doesn't fit the Beverly Hills mode, and Murphy manages to give the movie a little political charge as he resists this railroading hinting—at least to African American audiences—that he is channeling their experience.

Serious undercurrents aside, this is a movie in which Murphy is joyously uncontainable, thumbing his nose at the powers that be and putting bananas in their tail pipes until they have no choice but to go his way. That irresistible laugh opens doors as often as its irritates his opponents, and a combination of charm and outrageous lies get him in where other policemen fear to tread. This may not be as unfettered as in his stand-up classics, but it's Murphy near his best. He would have other hits, earning critical acclaim with *Bowfinger* and an Oscar nomination for *Dreamgirls*, but it's no slight to say that Axel Foley remains his signature role.

Opposite: Eddie Murphy as Detroit detective Axel Foley. Murphy was only 23 when he made this film, but already a four-year veteran of *Saturday Night Live*.

Above: Axel and Detective Billy Rosewood (Judge Reinhold) take cover while trading fire with the armed goons of bad guy Victor Maitland (Steven Berkoff).

ORIGINAL RELEASE DATE: December 5, 1984 (U.S.); January 25, 1985 (UK)
RUN TIME: 101 minutes

DID YOU KNOW?
◆ Martin Scorsese was approached to direct the film while Stallone was attached, but he thought the concept was too similar to Clint Eastwood's movie *Coogan's Bluff* and turned it down.

FURTHER VIEWING
◆ *The Golden Child* (1986)
Tony Scott's *Beverly Hills Cop II* does have its fans, amping up the action significantly, but give Murphy's odd fantasy/comedy *The Golden Child* a look. After all, how many other movies combine Tibetan Buddhism, a demonic Charles Dance, and airport security?

FACTS

THIS IS SPINAL TAP

1984

IT CLAIMS TO BE A DOCUMENTARY, OR "IF YOU WILL, A ROCKUMENTARY" IN THE WORDS OF "DIRECTOR" MARTY DIBERGI (DIRECTOR ROB REINER).

More accurately, it's a mockumentary, and a towering piece of comedy genius. You will struggle to find a professional comedian or musician who doesn't love it with a passion that borders on obsession, and a line of its dialogue is smuggled into everyday conversation approximately once a second, somewhere in the world. That's all the more impressive because almost none of those lines were scripted, instead growing out of a series of carefully imagined situations and beautifully developed characters.

Spinal Tap began in the 1960s, both in fiction and in fact. Christopher Guest and Michael McKean were students in New York City when they met and began playing music together. In 1978, they appeared on a series called The TV Show, with Harry Shearer and Rob Reiner, and played in a rock band for the first time. Quickly, Guest's Nigel Tufnel

and McKean's David St. Hubbins took shape, the pair of "fire and ice" British rockers behind Spinal Tap. That description comes from the band's third core member, Shearer, as the quieter and more philosophical bassist Derek Smalls ("I feel my role in the band is somewhere in the middle of that, like lukewarm water"), and the lineup was rounded off with a rotating cast of drummers.

It quickly became clear to Reiner that they had something special. The cast could play, they were funny, and the scene was ripe for satire. Even now, it's not immediately obvious to the unwary that Spinal Tap, a group named after a medical procedure, is any more implausible than, say, Iron Maiden, named after a medieval torture instrument. And their saga is really no more insane than that of real metal band Anvil, as recorded in 2008's nonmock

Above: The core Tap trio of Derek Smalls (Harry Shearer), Nigel Tufnel (Christopher Guest), and David St. Hubbins (Michael McKean) practice their pouts.

documentary *Anvil: The Story of Anvil*. The genre is so filled with absurdity that it should be beyond satire, yet the cast is talented enough as both musicians and comedians to make it work anyway.

Reiner quickly realized that a traditional script wasn't going to capture the tone they wanted, so they shot a short demo instead. Even with that visual evidence of the concept, no studio wanted to make *Tap*. It took legendary TV producer Norman Lear to see its potential and Peter Smokler, the veteran cameraman who'd worked on the rock doc *Gimme Shelter*, to give it the same feel as rock hits such as *The Last Waltz* (DiBergi was clearly modeled on Martin Scorsese's role as director and interrogator there).

To the extent that there is a plot, it is this: heavy metal group Spinal Tap, "one of England's loudest bands," has announced a new album and U.S. tour in fall 1982. Sometime commercial director Marty DiBergi follows them to chronicle "a hardworking band on the road." But disaster travels with them, from canceled concerts to insect pods that won't open to Stonehenge (a stage model that "was in danger of being crushed by a dwarf"). The band gets lost on their way from dressing room to stage; their meet 'n' greets completely lack fan presence;

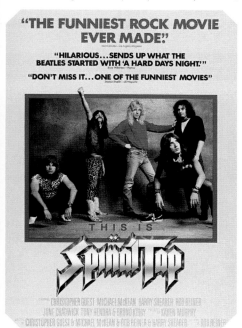

"THE FUNNIEST ROCK MOVIE EVER MADE."

"HILARIOUS...SENDS UP WHAT THE BEATLES STARTED WITH 'A HARD DAYS NIGHT.'"

"DON'T MISS IT...ONE OF THE FUNNIEST MOVIES"

THIS IS

Spinal Tap

CHRISTOPHER GUEST · MICHAEL McKEAN · HARRY SHEARER · ROB REINER
JUNE CHADWICK · TONY HENDRA & BRUNO KIRBY · KAREN MURPHY
CHRISTOPHER GUEST & MICHAEL McKEAN & ROB REINER & HARRY SHEARER · ROB REINER

ORIGINAL RELEASE DATE: March 2, 1984 (U.S.); May 4, 1984 (UK)
RUN TIME: 82 minutes

DID YOU KNOW?
◆ Rob Reiner asked Dire Straits's Mark Knopfler to score his 1987 movie *The Princess Bride*, but Knopfler agreed only on condition that Reiner hide his Spinal Tap baseball cap somewhere on-screen. It sits behind Fred Savage's bed.

FURTHER VIEWING
◆ *The Decline of Western Civilization* (1981) Penelope Spheeris's rock documentary and its first sequel (1988's *Part II*) offer a serious balance to *Tap*'s comedy, although the director went on to direct another iconic metal comedy, *Wayne's World*.

FACTS

they're billed beneath a puppet show. Tufnel and St. Hubbins's partnership is tested to the breaking point when their album turns out to be a disaster, and all their vainglorious posing is revealed as a sham. Just like the bulge in Smalls's pants.

One of the movie's best jokes is the ongoing tragedy of *Tap*'s drummers. There was the "bizarre gardening accident" that "the authorities said was best left unsolved"; the one who choked on someone else's vomit; the one who exploded onstage in a flash of green light; another who experienced spontaneous human combustion; and the one who disappeared in Japan along with the band's equipment and is either dead or playing jazz. Another nine are said to have died between 1970 and 1981. And yet volunteers keep signing up, trusting in the law of averages to protect them.

There is such a fine line between stupid and clever, yet *Spinal Tap* dances on that line like it's a vast stage. There's wordplay, there are astonishingly bad-taste gags (their "Smell the Glove" record cover, for one), and some of the best comic songs ever written. It killed the rock documentary for nearly two decades, because no band was confident that they could escape unflattering comparisons to *Tap*. But it also set Guest on a path to more mockumentary success (*Waiting for Guffman*, *A Mighty Wind*) and became a formative influence on nearly all modern comedy. From TV's *Modern Family* to *Borat*, *Spinal Tap* is still all around us.

Left: For many fans, the word "rock" in this poster quote is unnecessary.

A NIGHTMARE ON ELM STREET

1984

WE ARE VULNERABLE WHEN WE SLEEP.

An enemy could sneak up on us and we wouldn't have a chance to run; some disaster could kill us before we wake. But we still need to sleep, so we can function and for our very sanity. As this film's Dr. King says, "Everybody's got to dream, young lady." So the premise of Wes Craven's *A Nightmare on Elm Street*, a monster that can kill you in your dreams, holds a particular terror for every human being. After all, there is no way to avoid him, nowhere to run, and nowhere to hide inside your own mind—or whatever dreamworld this particular monster operates within.

The story starts as four teens realize they have shared a nightmare about a horrifically scarred figure with knives on his hands. Tina (Amanda Wyss) asks the others to stay over the next night in case it happens again, but she is killed in her dreams by something invisible. Her friend Nancy (Heather Langenkamp) knows that something is wrong, because she's having the same dreams. When Tina's boyfriend, and the chief suspect in her death, Rod (Nick Corri) is killed in his sleep, too, she's sure of it. As Nancy's dreams get worse, she realizes that her friend Glen (Johnny Depp) is also in the firing line— or perhaps that should be slashing line.

Nancy finally learns that her parents and other local residents may be responsible. Years before, they trapped a suspected child killer, Freddy Krueger (Robert Englund), after he escaped justice on a technicality, and they burned him to death. It is Krueger's ghost, or spirit, that is now seeking revenge in the dreamworld.

Despite the bizarre premise, a surprising amount of the movie was drawn from the real world. Kreuger's look was inspired by an old man who

Left: Freddy Krueger (Robert Englund), complete with horrifically burned face and steel-tipped murder gloves, haunts the dreams of the teenagers of Elm Street.

had frightened Craven as a child, and he was named after the director's childhood bully. The idea of a nightmare scaring someone to death was also drawn from reality; it had happened among Hmong refugees from the genocide in Laos. They had been too terrified to sleep and some had died without waking up, a phenomenon dubbed "sudden unexplained nocturnal death."

But it's the supernatural element, and the terrifyingly violent deaths, that give the movie its edge. Slashes open across Tina's chest without visible weapons; Rod is strangled by his own sheets. Glen has it worst of all. He suffers the final indignity of dying in a cropped shirt, pulled whole into his mattress before a veritable gusher of blood explodes out of the hole left behind to his mother's understandable horror. (As the paramedics arrive afterward, one cop says with black humor, "You don't need a stretcher up there; you need a mop.")

But amid uncaring parents and authority figures, the courageous Nancy fights back. She sets booby traps around her house and plots to pull Freddy into the real world to reduce his power. It's that sense of agency that makes Nancy one of the great horror heroines, even if her plan doesn't entirely work. She finds herself locked in a house with Krueger, and all her booby traps can't stop him.

The quality of effects is sometimes questionable. When Nancy is running upstairs only for the stairs to turn to quicksand beneath her, for example, you can see the holes where someone has cut through the tread. And compared to the sequels, where the dreamscapes became steadily more surreal and outrageous, these dreams are relatively mundane, based in recognizably everyday locations and without the surreal edge that is typical of dreams— at least until Fred (only Nancy calls him Freddy) Krueger strikes.

It is only when Nancy stops trying to fight Freddy and turns her back on him, denying him power over her, that he is finally defeated. Or is he? Nancy's vision of a happier next morning, with all her friends still alive and her mother more loving than ever, proves to be just another nightmare. It's never final with this character—even *The Final Nightmare* wasn't the last film in the series—and Freddy came back for one final scare. Oh, and eight more movies. The sequels were variable in quality and only Craven's efforts in *Dream Warriors* and *New Nightmare* really offer anything fresh beyond inventive and horrible deaths. But horrible deaths and buckets of blood are what we want to see, and *Nightmare*'s success ushered in a new era of similarly unrestrained, over-the-top supernatural slashers.

Left: The film's poster had to convey the nature of the dream attacks, but gave heroine Nancy (Heather Langenkamp) big hair and false nails to do it.

THE MOVIES YOU LOVED ...BACK THEN

If you were a child in the 1980s, chances are that you still stand by many of your favorite childhood movies, confident in the knowledge that they have been accepted as classics. However, some films have aged less well. You may have pestered your parents to take you to these movies, bought the sticker albums or tie-in books, but here are the movies that—in the cold light of adulthood—are pretty terrible.

KRULL (1983)

You may have fond memories of that floating Black Fortress and boomerang-style weapon "the Glaive" (which reappeared in *Ready Player One*), but return to Krull and you will find a tedious, somewhat pompous mess.

THE EWOK ADVENTURE: CARAVAN OF COURAGE (1984) AND EWOKS: THE BATTLE FOR ENDOR (1985)

These television movie spin-offs from *Star Wars: Return of the Jedi* see the adorable Ewoks meet two supremely annoying human kids, first helping them to find their missing parents and then—when their reunited family is mostly killed—helping the sole survivor find a new home.

THE CARE BEARS MOVIE (1985)

There's very little humor here for adults and a sense of glassy-eyed sentimentality that even kids may notice. One child character laughs, "Aren't parents great!"—something no small child has ever said. And the Care Bear stare is a little brainwash-y in retrospect.

MY LITTLE PONY: THE MOVIE (1986)

A bunch of pastel-colored ponies try to stop the advance of a giant purple ooze that makes its victims grumpy; it's not exactly *Die Hard*. With

a huge cast and unnecessarily complicated mythology, it's really just an extended toy ad.

TRANSFORMERS: THE MOVIE (1986)

They killed Optimus Prime in the opening act. Whatever followed, and however many cinephile points the movie gets for being the last credit for Orson Welles (voicing Unicron), there was no coming back from that.

BMX BANDITS (1983)

The title is so exciting, promising wild adventures despite its heroes (including a young Nicole Kidman) being too young for a driving license. And yet the movie is dry, and far more boring than a tale of kids vs. robbers has any right to be. Except for Kidman completists, best stick to *The Goonies*.

MANNEQUIN (1987)

You probably still love this, but it uses sexual harassment as a punchline and treats its only openly gay (and best) character, Hollywood Montrose, as a joke. Also, the whole being-in-love-with-a-dummy thing is super-super-creepy when you think about it.

SHORT CIRCUIT 2 (1988)

The first *Short Circuit* is pretty charming really, because Johnny 5 came alive and just wanted to learn stuff. The sequel, which has (white) Fisher Stevens in brownface as stereotyped Indian immigrant "Benjamin Jahveri," is more problematic.

MASTERS OF THE UNIVERSE (1987)

Another day, another movie based on a toy—although this one is live action for a change. It's still a cheap *Conan* wannabe, with the fate of Eternia dependent on a few Earth kids and Dolph Lundgren's leather bikini. And Frank Langella deserves better than the Skeletor makeup he suffers here.

MAC AND ME (1988)

One of the worst movies ever made, this is a cheap *E.T.* copycat that replaces charm and magic with McDonald's product placement. There is little to say in its favor, except that its wheelchair-using lead Eric (Jade Calegory) was at least played by a genuine wheelchair user in a rare moment of 1980s casting diversity.

BREAKIN' AND BREAKIN' 2: ELECTRIC BOOGALOO (1984)

Released only nine months apart, these two have great dance numbers but very little else to recommend them. *Breakin'* isn't terrible, although it makes the *Step Up* scripts look like art, but *Breakin' 2* is dull, lifeless stuff.

MICHAEL JACKSON'S MOONWALKER (1988)

Fans were hyped when they learned about a planned movie from the King of Pop. But if they went into *Moonwalker* expecting a story of any kind, they were soon to be disappointed. It's just a string of increasingly surreal music videos, climaxing with a Jackson-shaped rocket ship–robot.

Opposite: *Krull*, with its Black Fortress and the quest for the Glaive, may have seemed cool at the time, but it has aged very, very badly.

Below: Michael Jackson's *Moonwalker* turned out to be a very surreal collection of music videos rather than the pop adventure that younger fans had hoped for.

THE KARATE KID

1984

A BULLIED KID AND AN OLD MAN FORM AN UNLIKELY FRIENDSHIP IN THE BEST UNDERDOG TALE OF THE 1980S.

Left: Daniel LaRusso (Ralph Macchio) and Mr. Miyagi (Pat Morita) are wary as they visit the Cobra Kai dojo to challenge Johnny (William Zabka) and his friends to a match.

It came from the man who won an Oscar for directing *Rocky*, John G. Avildsen, though this underdog doesn't just go the distance: he wins the fight. That's how *The Karate Kid* has its cake and eats it. It talks about the importance of karate for balance and self-defense, but it also shows how cool it would be to be able to definitively beat the bullies, combining Eastern spirituality with good-old American competition.

Our hero is Daniel LaRusso (Ralph Macchio Jr.), who moves with his loving mom Lucille (Randee Heller) from New Jersey to Los Angeles. However, at his new school he is relentlessly bullied by rich, obnoxious Johnny Lawrence (William Zabka) and his outrageously Aryan buddies from the Cobra Kai karate dojo. The eccentric Mr. Miyagi (Noriyuki "Pat" Morita), superintendent of Daniel's apartment complex, stands up for his neighbor and eventually agrees to train Daniel to face his tormentors in a big karate tournament. His training methods, however, are unconventional.

That program is where we get the movie's famous "Wax on, wax off" mantra, with Mr. Miyagi subjecting Daniel to a series of apparently random chores: polishing cars, sanding floors, painting a fence. But, like a magician, it turns out that this hard labor has taught Daniel all the essential karate moves. All that's left is for him to pick up the film's famous "crane kick" (apparently, best practiced standing on a post on the beach), win the tournament, and get the girl (Elisabeth Shue's Ali).

What makes *Karate Kid* work is that it tackles its themes—bullying, single parenthood, the many pitfalls of young love—without patronizing its teenage protagonist. For example, Daniel claims he doesn't want to go to the school Halloween dance. However,

He taught him the secret to Karate lies in the mind and heart. Not in the hands.

The Karate Kid

COLUMBIA PICTURES Presents
A JERRY WEINTRAUB Production of A JOHN G. AVILDSEN Film
"THE KARATE KID"
Starring RALPH MACCHIO · NORIYUKI "PAT" MORITA · ELISABETH SHUE
Music by BILL CONTI Director of Photography BROOKS ARTHUR
Executive Producer R.J. LOUIS Written by ROBERT MARK KAMEN
Produced by JERRY WEINTRAUB Directed by JOHN G. AVILDSEN

when he admits he would go "if I went as the Invisible Man . . . so no one would see me," it becomes clear that it is bullies he's trying to avoid. It's heartbreaking to see the normally exuberant, even swaggering boy so hesitant, and heartwarming that, in the next scene, Mr. Miyagi has contrived an ingenious shower-cubicle costume for Daniel so he can dance safely with Ali. The young lovers—especially Daniel—also regularly mess up their relationship and have to apologize, which is also a good example.

Mr. Miyagi is sometimes skeptically viewed, not least because racist bullies mimicked his thick accent to mock people of Asian origin following the movie's success. But Pat Morita's funny, fierce character is no two-dimensional stereotype. This wise *sensei* is also a weirdo, and a proud immigrant (a fan of Detroit cars and Hawaiian shirts), a decorated war veteran, a grieving widower, and a bereaved father. He even touches on the great wrong that was the internment of Japanese Americans during World War II, so it's not just bonsai trees and getting drunk on sake. The movie also emphasizes Mr. Miyagi's moral commitment to the higher principles of karate, in contrast to militaristic Cobra Kai *sensei* John Kreese (Martin Kove), who teaches his

students that "Mercy is for the weak." But it's Kreese who ultimately shows fear; when he orders Daniel's semifinal opponent Bobby Brown (Ron Thomas) to put him out of action, and then tells Johnny to "sweep the leg," he seals their fate.

Wax on, wax off. Sweep the leg. It became one of the most quoted movies of the 1980s. Writer Robert Mark Kamen went on to create the *Taken* franchise, *The Fifth Element*, and *The Transporter*, but this remains his warmest and—one suspects—most personal story. He was even taught karate by "a funny little Okinawan man" who didn't believe in karate belts to mark progress, although there's no evidence that the inspiration had near-miraculous massage tricks.

The skinny, nervy Daniel and his bigger, blonder opponents look mismatched, even after all the training. But Daniel and Mr. Miyagi have heart and courage and humor on their side. Rocky secured only a pyrrhic victory, but Daniel's final crane kick is an unqualified triumph, the film finishing with Daniel hoisted in the air by cheering crowds and Mr. Miyagi simply smiling warmly. Daniel's victory includes important lessons about hard work, standing up to bullies without becoming an aggressor, and chasing balance instead of power. But it's also a story about the friendship, even surrogate fatherhood, between Mr. Miyagi and Daniel. "You're the best friend I ever had," says Daniel to his teacher on the eve of the competition. There's a tiny pause before Mr. Miyagi manages an understated reply: "You're pretty OK, too."

Left: On the poster, Daniel practices his "crane kick" in the Miyagi-approved seaside setting.

ORIGINAL RELEASE DATE: June 22, 1984 (U.S.); August 31, 1984 (UK)
RUN TIME: 122 minutes

DID YOU KNOW?
* Ralph Macchio still owns the film's canary-yellow 1947 Ford Super Deluxe Club Convertible.

FURTHER VIEWING
* *Police Story* (1985)
  If you want to see martial arts at the expert level, check out Jackie Chan's kung fu at its most physically dazzling in this, well, police story. It spawned a hugely successful franchise, thanks to unbelievable stunts.

FACTS

1985 HIGHLIGHTS

Back to the Future topped the box office, while Meryl Streep's accent ruled the Oscars. A gang of pensioners got a new lease of life thanks to a friendly alien visitation, while both of Sylvester Stallone's key action franchises—*Rocky* and *Rambo*—saw big-screen success. But the world said goodbye to Orson Welles, the genius who had gone from *Citizen Kane* to *Transformers: The Movie*.

HIGHEST-GROSSING FILMS (U.S.)

1. *Back to the Future*	Universal	$210,609,762
2. *Rambo: First Blood Part II*	TriStar	$150,415,432
3. *Rocky IV*	United Artists	$127,873,716
4. *The Color Purple*	Warner Bros.	$94,175,854
5. *Out of Africa*	Universal	$87,071,205
6. *Cocoon*	20th Century Fox	$76,113,124
7. *The Jewel of the Nile*	20th Century Fox	$75,973,200
8. *Witness*	Paramount	$68,706,993
9. *The Goonies*	Warner Bros.	$61,389,680
10. *Spies Like Us*	Warner Bros.	$60,088,980

AT THE GOLDEN GLOBES

Best Picture (Drama) — *Out of Africa*

Best Picture (Comedy/Musical) — *Prizzi's Honor*

Best Director — John Huston, *Prizzi's Honor*

Best Actor (Drama) — John Voigt, *Runaway Train*

Best Actor (Comedy/Musical) — Jack Nicholson, *Prizzi's Honor*

Best Actress (Drama) — Whoopi Goldberg, *The Color Purple*

Best Actress (Comedy/Musical) — Kathleen Turner, *Prizzi's Honor*

CANNES FILM FESTIVAL

Palme d'Or winner

When Father Was Away on Business, Emir Kusturica

NOTABLE DEATHS

Louise Brooks, August 8 — Actor, *Pandora's Box* and *Diary of a Lost Girl*

Rock Hudson, October 2 — Actor, *Giant* and *Pillow Talk*

Yul Brynner, October 10 — Actor, *The King and I* and *The Magnificent Seven*

Orson Welles, October 10 — Actor/director, *Citizen Kane* and *The Magnificent Ambersons*

Sam Spiegel, December 31 — Producer, *Lawrence of Arabia* and *On the Waterfront*

AT THE OSCARS

Best Picture — *Out of Africa*

Best Director — Sydney Pollack, *Out of Africa*

Best Actor — William Hurt, *Kiss of the Spider Woman*

Best Actress — Geraldine Page, *The Trip to Bountiful*

THIS YEAR'S BIG OSCARS INJUSTICE

Steven Spielberg's *The Color Purple* was nominated for 11 awards and went home empty-handed, making it the joint most-snubbed film in Oscars history. They couldn't even spare one?

FUTURE MOVIE STAR BIRTHS

March 26: Keira Knightley, *Atonement* and *Pirates of the Caribbean*

May 28: Carey Mulligan, *An Education* and *Inside Llewyn Davis*

June 12: Dave Franco, *Neighbors* and *The Disaster Artist*

August 9: Anna Kendrick, *Up in the Air* and *Pitch Perfect*

December 3: Amanda Seyfried, *Mean Girls* and *Mamma Mia!*

NOTABLE FILM DEBUTS

Don Cheadle, *Moving Violations*

Whoopi Goldberg, *The Color Purple*

Madonna, *Vision Quest*

Viggo Mortensen, *Witness*

River Phoenix, *Explorers*

Keanu Reeves, *One Step Away*

BACK TO THE FUTURE

1985

SOME MOVIES WEAR THEIR GREATNESS SO LIGHTLY THAT YOU COULD ALMOST MISS IT.

They don't grasp for awards or claim weighty subject matter, and yet their influence is more enduring and their message is often more powerful. *Back to the Future* is one such movie, in which every movement is so beautifully in sync that the dance looks effortless and light as a feather. There isn't a wasted moment or bad line, and while it may all seem fun and frothy, it was the result of hard and heavy work.

The script, by director Robert Zemeckis and his writing partner Bob Gale, sat unwanted for four years. Forty-four executives around Tinseltown rejected it, and then Zemeckis's success as a director-for-hire on *Romancing the Stone* put him in a position to name his next movie. He went back to bat for *Back to the Future*, with support from his old collaborator Steven

Above: The time machine in *Back to the Future* was originally a laser, and then a fridge. But director Robert Zemeckis reasoned that you'd want to be mobile geographically as well as chronologically, and chose the futuristic-looking DeLorean gull-wing car.

Left: Michael J. Fox replaced Eric Stoltz as Marty McFly several weeks into filming.

Spielberg (Zemeckis and Gale wrote Spielberg's disastrous *1941*, but they gelled despite that) and finally got the green light. Even then, the movie went through profound changes to become a classic.

We all know the story that made it. Michael J. Fox's Marty McFly travels thirty years back through time in his friend Doc Brown's (Christopher Lloyd) DeLorean-turned-time-machine. There, he accidentally stops his parents from meeting, so he must put history back on track to save his own life while the younger Doc labors to fix his ride and send him back—to the future. Oh, and he invents rock 'n' roll while he's at it, in a scene that was designed as a throwaway gag but now looks unfortunately like cultural appropriation.

And it almost didn't happen. For the first four weeks of shooting, Eric Stoltz played Marty, but he just couldn't find the light, comic tone needed (although by all accounts he gave a dramatic performance that would have been fine in any other movie). Zemeckis had originally wanted Fox, but the actor was committed to the TV sitcom *Family Ties*. Still, he asked again, and the actor was so eager after reading the script that he agreed to do both jobs at once. Fox would rehearse and shoot his TV role by day, report to the movie set by night, and squeeze all the movie's exterior shots into the weekends. It was exhausting, but he was smart enough to spot a dream job.

Meanwhile, John Lithgow had been the first choice for Doc Brown, who was originally a professor, but he was also busy, so it went to Christopher Lloyd. It took the writers ages to work out how to gracefully and in a noncringing way resolve the question of Marty's young mother's crush on her time-traveling son (they came up with "Ugh, it's like kissing my brother" and everyone breathed a sigh of relief). At one point, the time machine was a refrigerator, an idea crushed because Zemeckis and Gale were worried that kids would copy the movie and get stuck. The original ending had Marty drive into a nuclear test site to time-travel home—thankfully, it was outside the final budget—and it was almost called *Spacemen from Pluto* after producer Sid Sheinberg complained that no movie with the word "future" in the title ever made money.

ORIGINAL RELEASE DATE: July 3, 1985 (U.S.); December 4, 1985 (UK)
RUN TIME: 116 minutes

DID YOU KNOW?

- The "Johnny B. Goode" performance was almost cut at the eleventh hour and was kept in only after test audiences went mad for it.
- It would take 484 wind turbines to produce the 1.21 gigawatts necessary for time travel.

FURTHER VIEWING

- *Bill and Ted's Excellent Adventure* (1989)
The *other* great '80s time-travel comedy introduced us to Alex Winter's Bill S. Preston Esq. and Keanu Reeves's Ted "Theodore" Logan (together, they are "Wyld Stallyns"!).

FACTS

That was about to change. The movie was set for an August release, the time of year when studios dump oddities and risks, but the test screenings were wildly successful, so the release was pushed up to the Fourth of July weekend, the ultimate American date for a movie steeped in Americana. *Back to the Future* spent eleven weeks at the top of the U.S. box office and became a pop culture touchstone.

Two sequels followed, shot back-to-back and released in 1989 and 1990. Critical opinion on those varies. *Part II* was judged overly complex and dark at the time—although it now looks uncomfortably prophetic in its vision of a despotic, corrupt American future—while *Part III*'s Western antics were better liked on release but found, perhaps, lacking substance in the end.

However, there is no argument about the original. It is an elegant philosophical illustration of the grandfather paradox, an enduring portrait of small-town American values, and—on top of all that—an absolute joy to watch. Fox's hangdog-underdog Marty is ferociously likable; Doc adds a manic energy ("Great Scott!") and Marty's poor parents-to-be are adorably clueless. The only real letdown is that we're well past 2015, and cars still don't fly. But as "comedy-adventure-science-speculation-coming-of-age-rock-and-roll-time-travel-period films" go, as Zemeckis dubbed it, it's the best there's ever been.

THE GOONIES

1985

WHAT IS IT ABOUT *THE GOONIES*? IT IS, ALMOST WITHOUT FAIL, THE FIRST MOVIE MENTIONED WHENEVER A GROUP OF 80S KIDS GATHERS TO REMINISCE.

Perhaps there is magic in its blend of wild adventure and pint-size heroes, and in the idea that we could all be Indiana Jones if only we got on our bikes and rode away with our best friends. There's pirate treasure waiting, and a gang of unpopular kids can find it with the right blend of luck, pluck, and every swear word. The story is set in Astoria, Oregon, a small town perpetually on the verge of rain. A heartless developer plans to foreclose on homes in the Goon Docks neighborhood to build a golf course, much to the dismay of the local kids. Just before these "Goonies" are scattered to the four winds, young Mikey Walsh (Sean Astin) discovers a pirate's map in the attic and sets off in search of the treasure that could save his home. He's accompanied by his older brother Brand (Josh Brolin), manic friend Mouth (Corey Feldman), would-be inventor Data (Jonathan Ke Quan), the stunningly clumsy Chunk (Jeff Cohen), and two cooler, older high school girls, Andy (Kerri Green) and Stef (Martha Plimpton).

The unlikely gang must navigate an underground labyrinth filled with booby traps and puzzles to solve a quest laid down centuries before by the dread pirate One-Eyed Willie (a double entendre that never fails to amuse British viewers). Standing in their way are a fugitive criminal gang, Mama Fratelli (Anne Fletcher) and her sons Jake (Robert Davi) and Francis (Joe Pantoliano). These are not the sympathetic villains we see in overwritten modern blockbusters, spurred on by some tragedy in the past or corrupted by a cruel world. These are fabulously pantomime, merrily murderous baddies. They sneer ("Kids suck!" spits the unmotherly Mama), take hostages, and stalk after the kids to

claim the pirate's gold.

As a plot, it's faintly generic, like a *Scooby-Doo* episode stretched out to feature length. Then again, that familiarity roots it in a tradition of children's adventure that goes all the way back to *Treasure Island*, via *Our Gang* and *Annie*. But it's the characters that shine; these kids feel eccentric and rounded and real as they bicker, swear, and talk over one another. Our hero, Mikey, muddles his words when he gets excited and has asthma, yet can still deliver a rousing speech when the moment comes. Mouth can be obnoxious—watch him torment Mikey's housekeeper in Spanish—but he has a vulnerable

Above: Mike (Sean Astin), Brand (Josh Brolin) and Data (Jonathan Ke Quan) make a nasty discovery while on the hunt for pirate treasure.

Opposite: The physically unfeasible but wildly exciting poster image of the Goonies gang.

side that is barely concealed by his chatter. Even Data is more than a one-joke gimmick; his reunion with his dad has heart. And Chunk plays a crucial role in rescuing them all.

The movie's secret weapon, however, is a grown man. Played by former NFL star John Matuszak under heavy prosthetics, the tragically deformed Sloth looks terrifying, but he proves to be the most valiant and caring of all the Goonies. His cheerful battle cry of "Hey, you guys!" is still quoted daily around the world, and the sight of this supposed monster, proudly posing in his Superman shirt before swinging to the rescue, makes the most cynical heart soar.

It's a compliment rather than a criticism to note that this movie is a career highlight for few of those involved. Director Richard Donner had already made *Superman* and would go on to *Lethal Weapon* and *Scrooged*. Screenwriter Chris Columbus would direct the first two Harry Potter movies and write *Home Alone*, while Steven Spielberg also produced a better movie that year—*Back to the Future*—never mind his untouchable directing career. Even those young stars largely went on to bigger and better things, such as *The Lord of the Rings* (Astin), *Parenthood* (Plimpton), *Stand by Me* (Feldman), and *No Country for Old Men* (Brolin).

However, as a convergence of talent, brought together in the right place at the right time, it's unbeatable. The kids are so expressive that it could be a silent movie, yet the dialogue sparkles too much to lose ("That says 1632; is that a year or something?" asks Chunk of the treasure map). The sometimes-ropey effects match the *Looney Tunes* feel to the whole adventure (listen for a traditional cartoon "sprooooooooing" sound effect when Data deploys his "Pinchers of Peril") and suit the young kids improvising their way out of danger.

If that treasure-hunting plot is familiar, the characters are full of surprises. The monster turns out to be a hero, the fat comic relief saves the day, and the gasping, sensitive kid in double denim emerges as the undisputed leader of the whole bunch. It's these underdog characters that inspired our love of *The Goonies*, and they still inspire viewers

to never say die. The movie's flaws don't really matter amid such riches, because, to quote its Cyndi Lauper theme song, "Goonies are good enough."

ORIGINAL RELEASE DATE: June 7, 1985 (U.S.); November 29, 1985 (UK)
RUN TIME: 113 minutes

DID YOU KNOW?

* The Astoria police chief accuses Chunk of making a prank call about "all those little creatures that multiply when you throw water on them"—a reference to *Gremlins*, which was also produced by Spielberg and starred Feldman.

FURTHER VIEWING

* *Explorers* (1985)
  Ethan Hawke and River Phoenix star as kids who build a blueprint for a spaceship and find themselves on an exhilarating alien adventure.

FACTS

THE BRAT PACK

It defined a certain type of 1980s movie—but what exactly
was the Brat Pack? Where did the name come from?

In 1985, *New York* magazine published a cover story
about *The Breakfast Club* and *St. Elmo's Fire*, and
dubbed the young stars of those movies the "Brat
Pack," a riff on Frank Sinatra's 1960s "Rat Pack."
The gang centered on Emilio Estevez, star of both
movies and Demi Moore's fiancé at the time, but
it grew to encompass a generation, enfolding the
cast of *The Outsiders* (alongside Estevez again) and

the likes of James Spader, Robert Downey Jr., and
Charlie Sheen. The group rejected the nickname,
with Estevez, Rob Lowe, and Judd Nelson claiming
that it held them back from more serious adult roles
and Ally Sheedy saying that it destroyed their easy
camaraderie. However, they are all still working in
Hollywood thirty years later, so the Brat Pack gets
the last laugh. Let's take a look at the core eight:

Above: Judd Nelson, Emilio
Estevez, Ally Sheedy, Molly
Ringwald, and Anthony Michael
Hall in *The Breakfast Club*, one
of the founding Brat Pack films.

EMILIO ESTEVEZ
BORN: 1962
STARRED IN: *THE BREAKFAST CLUB, THE OUTSIDERS,
ST. ELMO'S FIRE, STAKEOUT, YOUNG GUNS*

The son of Martin Sheen, Estevez seemed to arrive on the scene a completely formed movie star, his persona all swagger on top and vulnerability underneath. If there was a godfather of the Brat Pack, it was Estevez, who was briefly engaged to Demi Moore.

POST–BRAT PACK CAREER

A string of early 1990s hits, including *Stakeout*, *The Mighty Ducks*, and *Young Guns*, suggested Estevez might go all the way. But he shunned publicity and stepped back from acting, forging a new career as a director of movies: *Bobby* (2006) and *The Way* (2011).

MOLLY RINGWALD
BORN: 1968
STARRED IN: *THE BREAKFAST CLUB, SIXTEEN CANDLES, PRETTY IN PINK,
THE PICK-UP ARTIST* (WITH DOWNEY), *FRESH HORSES* (WITH MCCARTHY)

John Hughes's muse had—inevitably, given that glorious red hair—begun her acting career onstage as Annie. In her great teen movies, she had an indefinable everyday quality, a combination of teen sulkiness and optimism that rings true.

POST–BRAT PACK CAREER

Ringwald, struggling to shrug off typecasting, moved to France to work there before returning to her musical roots. By the 2000s, she embraced her legacy with knowing turns in *Not Another Teen Movie* and television shows such as *Riverdale*.

ANTHONY MICHAEL HALL
BORN: 1968
STARRED IN: *THE BREAKFAST CLUB, SIXTEEN CANDLES, WEIRD SCIENCE,
NATIONAL LAMPOON'S VACATION, HAIL CAESAR* (WITH NELSON AND DOWNEY)

The Breakfast Club's "geek" played variations on that role to perfection three times, but he tried to avoid being typecast, turning down roles written specifically for him in *Pretty in Pink* (Ducky) and *Ferris Bueller's Day Off* (Cameron).

POST–BRAT PACK CAREER

Hall joined *Saturday Night Live*'s cast to show his range and took two years off to battle a drinking problem before returning to play a bully in 1990's *Edward Scissorhands*. As an adult, he's had well-received roles in *Pirates of Silicon Valley* and *The Dark Knight*.

ROB LOWE
BORN: 1964
STARRED IN: *ST. ELMO'S FIRE, THE OUTSIDERS,
ABOUT LAST NIGHT*

The most preposterously handsome of the bunch, Lowe's roles in *St. Elmo's Fire* and *About Last Night* saw him confined to romantic leads for much of the 1980s, until his career was derailed by not one but two sex tape scandals.

POST–BRAT PACK CAREER

By the 1990s, Lowe found redemption in comedy, poking fun at himself in *Wayne's World* and *Austin Powers*, and truly hitting his stride on television with *The Stand* (with Ringwald), in *The West Wing*, and as the perky Chris Traeger in *Parks and Recreation*.

ANDREW MCCARTHY

BORN: 1962
STARRED IN: *ST. ELMO'S FIRE, PRETTY IN PINK, MANNEQUIN, LESS THAN ZERO, HEAVEN HELP US, WEEKEND AT BERNIE'S*

Always a reluctant member of the club, McCarthy rejected the Brat Pack label almost immediately. However, he had one of the most successful 1980s careers of the lot, culminating in the cult hit *Weekend at Bernie's*.

POST–BRAT PACK CAREER

Since fighting alcoholism in 1992, McCarthy stepped away from acting and into travel writing for *National Geographic*. He's also a successful television director, with credits including *Orange Is the New Black* and *The Blacklist*, with old sparring buddy James Spader.

JUDD NELSON

BORN: 1959
STARRED IN: *THE BREAKFAST CLUB, ST. ELMO'S FIRE, BLUE CITY* (WITH ALLY SHEEDY), *NEVER ON TUESDAY* (WITH ESTEVEZ AND SHEEN)

The Breakfast Club finishes with the iconic image of Nelson's Bender punching the air to the sound of Simple Minds, and perhaps it would be unfair to expect any career to live up to that. Still, he did voice Rodimus Prime in *Transformers: The Movie*.

POST–BRAT PACK CAREER

Appearances in *New Jack City*, *Airheads*, and more meant that Nelson has worked pretty consistently. He is found more often on television in recent years, notably in *Empire* (where Moore has also been guesting), but he's never quit acting.

DEMI MOORE

BORN: 1962
STARRED IN: *ST. ELMO'S FIRE, ABOUT LAST NIGHT*

Moore was definitely a member of the Brat Pack, there in the main cast of *St. Elmo's Fire* and briefly engaged to Emilio Estevez. *About Last Night* was the best indication of what she should do at the time, blending potent charm and high drama perfectly.

POST–BRAT PACK CAREER

By the 1990s Moore was the biggest star of the lot, when *Ghost*, *A Few Good Men*, and *Indecent Proposal* made her the highest-paid actress in Hollywood and she caused a scandal by appearing nude and pregnant on the cover of *Vanity Fair*. Performances like her turn in *Margin Call* stand as a reminder of her acting talent.

ALLY SHEEDY

BORN: 1962
STARRED IN: *THE BREAKFAST CLUB, ST. ELMO'S FIRE, WARGAMES, SHORT CIRCUIT*

Initially, Sheedy seemed to shake off the Brat logo and transition into other movies more easily than her fellows, taking likable roles in *WarGames* and *Short Circuit*. She escaped stereotyping as a "basket case," and often played the popular, cool girl.

POST–BRAT PACK CAREER

Sheedy battled an addiction to sleeping pills in the 1990s before coming back to indie success in Lisa Cholodenko's *High Art* and a second career on Broadway. You may have missed her tiny cameo in *X-Men: Apocalypse*, but she has also appeared opposite Anthony Michael Hall in TV's *The Dead Zone*.

Above: Rob Lowe, Emilio Estevez, Judd Nelson, Andrew McCarthy, Mare Winningham, Demi Moore, and Ally Sheedy reunited the gang in *St. Elmo's Fire*.

Inset: Ringwald and Andrew McCarthy had another hit, alongside Jon Cryer, in *Pretty in Pink*.

THE BREAKFAST CLUB

PRIOR TO THE ARRIVAL OF JOHN HUGHES, TEENS HAD IT PRETTY TOUGH IN THE MOVIES.

Left: The quintet of Brat Pack characters in *The Breakfast Club* established teen archetypes that are still used liberally today.

They had first been recognized as an independent generation in the 1950s with the movie *Rebel Without a Cause*, but moviemakers were slow to figure out how to talk to or about them. The Moral Majority railed against any depiction of teen rebellion or "bad" behavior, but the alternatives offered included all those sanitized beach party movies of the 1960s starring Frankie Avalon and Annette Funicello. A few movies in the 1970s managed to walk a line by setting their stories in the past, allowing them to include a little more sex and booze—think *Grease* or *American Graffiti*—but it wasn't until *The Breakfast Club*, Hughes's second movie, that teens were listened to, and represented as more than clichés, on the big screen.

Looking back, what's remarkable about *The Breakfast Club* is what it is not. It's a teen movie without a prom, without a big game, without an inspirational teacher. It doesn't have a pep rally or a crowded cafeteria. It isn't a sex comedy full of voyeuristic scenes of young people showering together, nor is there a monster of any kind picking off the kids one by one. Instead, it's one of the most quietly revolutionary movies of the 1980s, opening the door to a thousand teen dramas and arguably much of young adult fiction.

There is nothing so structured as a plot. "A brain, an athlete, a basket case, a princess, and a criminal" are all sentenced to Saturday detention, arriving at seven o'clock in the morning for a nine-hour stretch. It's a big school and they're basically strangers, familiar to one another by sight at best. They're tasked with writing a thousand-word essay on the topic of "Who do you think you are?" but initially they squabble, tease one another, and try to get in a quick nap. Still, somewhere between having lunch and getting stoned, they start talking honestly to one another about their feelings and families, and break down some of the social walls that have divided them.

When the group does start talking, first through bantering challenges ("What would you do for a million dollars?") and then through more sincere questions ("What's wrong with you? Why don't you like yourself?"), it quickly becomes clear that they have more in common than they realized. Claire (Molly Ringwald) may be pretty and popular, but she's also used as an emotional football between her estranged parents. Andrew (Emilio Estevez) may be a sports success, but he's pressured into it by parents who seem to care more about his role on the team than his happiness. Pressure is also familiar to Brian (Andrew Michael Hall), although it's academic success his family wants, while John Bender (Judd Nelson) and Allison (Ally Sheedy) are, respectively, abused and ignored by their parents. Allison's the one who says, "My home life is unsatisfying," but she could be speaking for any of them.

There are admittedly weird touches to this movie that make it memorable. Allison draws a lovely pen sketch of a covered bridge, and then rubs her head to make it "snow" dandruff over the drawing. Claire draws stares with her fancy-pants sushi lunch; Andrew eats enough for all five of them, and Bender has brought nothing. Bender whistles the "Colonel Bogey March," used by the Allied prisoners in The Bridge on the River Kwai, and the others join in to taunt Assistant Principal Vernon (Paul Gleason), their dismissive teacher. For some reason, when this group gets stoned, they become extremely hyper and dance around the library instead of collapsing into a stupor or disappearing in search of cookies.

There are also nasty moments, although in that respect this movie has aged considerably better than Hughes's previous effort, Sixteen Candles. Bender's open hostility to Claire goes too far into abuse for modern audiences to be comfortable watching a romance later blossom between them; calling someone out on their comforting delusions is one thing, but his campaign against her feels sadistic. And the movie becomes awkward when it tries to play a grand romantic beat between Andrew and (a made-over) Allison. "I don't want to be alone anymore," she says. "You don't have to be," he answers. It feels overblown, like they're parroting lines from a movie, but perhaps they are, and that stiffness is deliberate. These kids are trying to figure out themselves, their families, and life itself, and they are mimicking friends, parents, or the wider world until they find their own way. The difference between The Breakfast Club and everything before it is that Hughes took that quest seriously, and he took teenagers as seriously as they take themselves. It changed teen movies forever.

ORIGINAL RELEASE DATE: February 15, 1985 (U.S.); June 7, 1985 (UK)
RUN TIME: 93 minutes

DID YOU KNOW?
+ Hughes's original cut was closer to two and a half hours and included a dream sequence in which Allison imagined the others as a Viking (Andrew), bride (Claire), prisoner (Bender), and an astronaut (Brian). She saw herself as a vampire.

FURTHER VIEWING
+ *Pretty in Pink* (1986)
  John Hughes wrote but did not direct this quirky love triangle drama, in which Molly Ringwald plays a girl with terrible taste in men who is so talented in fashion that she can turn two nice dresses into one hideous one.

FACTS

1986 HIGHLIGHTS

Film took a highway to the danger zone, only to find an Australian guy with a big knife hanging around. Ripley returned to LV-426 in *Aliens*, while Charlie Sheen ventured onto killing fields almost as dangerous in Oliver Stone's *Platoon*. Paul Newman picked up a long overdue Oscar, and Captain Kirk saved the whales.

HIGHEST-GROSSING FILMS (U.S.)

1. *Top Gun*	Paramount	$176,781,728
2. *Crocodile Dundee*	Paramount	$174,803,506
3. *Platoon*	Orion Pictures	$138,530,565
4. *The Karate Kid Part II*	Columbia	$115,103,979
5. *Star Trek IV: The Voyage Home*	Paramount	$109,713,132
6. *Back to School*	Orion	$91,258,000
7. *Aliens*	20th Century Fox	$86,160,248
8. *The Golden Child*	Paramount	$79,817,937
9. *Ruthless People*	Walt Disney Pictures	$71,624,879
10. *Ferris Bueller's Day Off*	Paramount	$70,136,169

AT THE GOLDEN GLOBES

Best Picture (Drama)	*Platoon*
Best Picture (Comedy/Musical)	*Hannah and Her Sisters*
Best Director	Oliver Stone, *Platoon*
Best Actor (Drama)	Bob Hoskins, *Mona Lisa*
Best Actor (Comedy/Musical)	Paul Hogan, *Crocodile Dundee*
Best Actress (Drama)	Marlee Matlin, *Children of a Lesser God*
Best Actress (Comedy/Musical)	Sissy Spacek, *Crimes of the Heart*

CANNES FILM FESTIVAL

Palme d'Or winner
The Mission, Roland Joffe

NOTABLE DEATHS

Donna Reed, January 14	Actor, *It's a Wonderful Life* and *From Here to Eternity*
James Cagney, March 30	Actor, *White Heat* and *Angels with Dirty Faces*
Scatman Crothers, November 22	Actor and musician, *The Shining* and *One Flew Over the Cuckoo's Nest*
Cary Grant, November 29	Actor, *His Girl Friday* and *North by Northwest*
Andrei Tarkovsky, December 28	Director, *Solaris* and *Andrei Rublev*

AT THE OSCARS

Best Picture	*Platoon*
Best Director	Oliver Stone, *Platoon*
Best Actor	Paul Newman, *The Color of Money*
Best Actress	Marlee Matlin, *Children of a Lesser God*

THIS YEAR'S BIG OSCARS INJUSTICE

In the Best Score category, Herbie Hancock's *Round Midnight* score beat the much-better-remembered Ennio Morricone score for *The Mission* and James Horner's pared-back *Aliens* score.

FUTURE MOVIE STAR BIRTHS

May 13: Robert Pattinson, *Twilight* and *Good Time*
May 16: Megan Fox, *Transformers* and *Jennifer's Body*
June 12: Shia LaBeouf, *Transformers* and *American Honey*
July 2: Lindsay Lohan, *Mean Girls* and *The Parent Trap*
August 28: Armie Hammer, *The Social Network* and *Call Me by Your Name*

NOTABLE FILM DEBUTS

Christian Bale, *Anastasia: The Mystery of Anna*
Jennifer Lopez, *My Little Girl*
Joaquin Phoenix, *Space Camp*
Winona Ryder, *Lucas*
Kristin Scott Thomas, *Under the Cherry Moon*
Wesley Snipes, *Wildcats*

TOP GUN

1986

FEW 1980S MOVIES SUM UP THE DECADE'S EXCESS, BOUNDLESS SELF-CONFIDENCE, OR REAGANITE FOREIGN POLICY BETTER THAN *TOP GUN*.

Fighter pilots are famously cocksure even at their most self-effacing; those at Miramar's "Top Gun" academy are supposed to be the best of the best, and therefore this is a story of characters whose egos are roughly the size of the aircraft carriers on which they land. But their self-belief is so overwhelming that it never occurs to the average viewer to doubt them. No wonder the movie launched Tom Cruise to the heights of fame at which he has remained ever since, and it took Tony Scott from "interesting newcomer" to established name.

To the extent that there is a plot, it's the story of Cruise's Pete "Maverick" Mitchell and his quest to land first place at the U.S. Navy's Top Gun academy with the help of natural flying ability and a megawatt smile. To do so, he'll have to overcome Val Kilmer's technically perfect Tom "Ice Man" Kazansky and—more pressingly—his own father complex, due to the lingering disgrace of his dad's apparent screw-up during the Vietnam War. Amid all this, he falls in love with a civilian instructor on the program, Charlotte "Charlie" Blackwood (Kelly McGillis), and he has to cope with the devastating loss of his Radar Intercept Officer and best friend Nick "Goose" Bradshaw (Anthony Edwards).

The movie was inspired by a 1983 magazine article about "Fightertown USA" and its inhabitants; it went through numerous script drafts at the behest of producers Don Simpson and Jerry Bruckheimer, who knew they were on to something before it reached the screen. The producers also had to involve the U.S. Navy to get their cooperation in planes and equipment, which meant making sure that the story met with Navy approval. That's

Left: Due to a three-inch difference in height, Tom Cruise had to wear platform shoes when standing in scenes with Kelly McGillis.

when Charlie switched from being a fellow officer to a civilian consultant, because of rules against fraternization, and the "enemy" they face became a nebulous opponent instead of a specific country. Of course, suggestions that briefings are not typically held in aircraft hangars next to runways were met with less receptiveness, because Scott and his producers knew how the movie was meant to look, and reality—past a certain point—be damned.

In the end, the story of the movie is incidental to its feel, as if Tony Scott set out to make the muscular American version of all those style-over-substance French movies of the same decade known as *cinéma du look*. The romance became a significant thread of the film, softening it and drawing in viewers who have no time for action but a lot of time for handsome men in dress whites. It helps that Charlie's a character who gives as good as she gets, shooting Maverick down hard the first time he hits on her and making it clear that she is no pushover (while also being bowled over by him, admittedly). But the rest of the movie is almost pure machismo. There are speeding cars, motorcycles, and, of course, fighter jets. There are manly men in flight suits, and stripped to the waist to oil themselves up (apparently) and play a not-so-friendly game of volleyball. And there are dogfights high above the desert and over the ocean, thrilling portrayals of flying that make it look like the next best thing to heaven.

And at last, Maverick overcomes his father issues, with the help of some classified information from chief instructor Viper (Tom Selleck), who reveals the truth about the elder Mitchell's death. "Is that why you fly the way you do? Trying to prove something? Yeah, your old man did it right." Of course, Maverick's ability is genetically ordained, and, of course, he needed to come to terms with his father's death to fulfill his own destiny. Unfortunately, every Tom Cruise character for the next ten years would have to repeat the same process.

The film is all beautifully pulled together by Tony Scott and full of cool moments. These pilots somehow intimidate the enemy just by outflying them or hovering upside down directly above them, giving them the finger. They have cool nicknames

ORIGINAL RELEASE DATE: May 16, 1986 (U.S.); October 3, 1986 (UK)
RUN TIME: 105 minutes

DID YOU KNOW?

- Charlie's friend Perry, in the bar scene in which Maverick tries to pick her up, is played by real-life Top Gun instructor Rear Admiral Pete Pettigrew, a technical consultant on the film.

FURTHER VIEWING

- *Rain Man* (1989)
  Top Gun made Tom Cruise a star, but the first movie that really showed the extent of his acting ability was *Rain Man*, in which he plays a selfish yuppie who discovers he has a long-lost autistic brother (Dustin Hoffman).

FACTS

such as Cougar, Merlin, and Sundown, and say things like "Too close for missiles; I'm switching to guns." Their egos write checks their bodies can't cash; they buzz control towers and promise never to abandon their wingman. The militaristic excess of this movie established a model that still shapes moviemakers such as Michael Bay and Peter Berg, but few of its would-be imitators can match the energy or style of *Top Gun*.

Below: Tom Cruise straps in and prepares to take the highway to the danger zone.

ALIENS

1986

IT'S A BRAVE DIRECTOR WHO PITCHES A SEQUEL TO ONE OF THE BEST-REGARDED MOVIES OF ALL TIME AND SWITCHES ITS GENRE.

However, James Cameron has never lacked guts. While still working on *The Terminator*, he was offered the chance to take the reins of a sequel to Ridley Scott's 1979 masterpiece *Alien*. Cameron's pitch was an action movie take on the original haunted-house-in-space premise, as a gung-ho military squad is sent to tackle the alien menace. It's a brilliant sequel, both faithful to and entirely different from the original, and a stunning action movie in its own right.

The sole survivor of the *Nostromo*, Sigourney Weaver's Ellen Ripley, is still the heart of the story. Her rescue pod has been found, but after fifty-seven years in space, she returns to an unfamiliar world and finds herself scapegoated for her ship's destruction. Weyland-Yutani's Carter Burke (Paul Reiser) patronizes her amicably, and that's the best of it. Her story is generally dismissed and her warnings ignored. Until, that is, a few months later, when transmissions from the Hadley's Hope colony established on LV-426, the world the *Nostromo* crew explored, abruptly cease. Ripley is called back to advise the Colonial Marines who are sent to investigate, eliminate any threat, and salvage as much of the colony as possible. "C'mon, it's a second chance, kiddo," urges Burke with all the bonhomie he can manufacture.

The threat comes, of course, from the xenomorphs, the acid-blooded killers of Scott's movie. But this time the victims are prepared, or think they are. With heavy weapons and years of training, the Marines virtually strut onto the planet from the USS *Sulaco*, confident in their firepower. "I only need to know one thing: where they are," claims Vasquez (Jenette Goldstein), and there is a supremely martial muster scene as they check weapons, prep their tank, and

drop to the planet's surface. They are smart, well-trained, and execute a tactically sound entry to the colony. What could possibly go wrong?

Pride goeth before a fall. This is a post-Vietnam movie, the technologically superior force taken down by a guerrilla opponent. From Vasquez's confidence we quickly slide to the jittering panic of Hudson's, "Game over, man, game over!" Disaster strikes in their first encounter with the aliens. The squad can't use their full firepower, because of

Below: Sigourney Weaver and Carrie Henn prepare to face down a horde of bloodthirsty xenomorphs.

H. R. Giger's unforgettable design) is one of the great horror revelations. Ripley threatens her with a flamethrower, and the queen calls her drones off—but when Ripley burns the egg field behind her, the queen makes it personal.

In the hands of a righteous woman, all that firepower (flamethrower, grenade launcher, machine gun) finally comes in useful. It takes almost hand-to-hand combat to finally kill the queen and end the alien threat—even after Ripley, Hicks, and Newt take off and, as our heroine originally advised, nuke the site from orbit.

There were other *Alien* movies after *Aliens*, but only this has completely lived up to the standard of the first film. Cameron's propulsive action style clicked smoothly in against Scott's nightmare scenario, and he carried over enough of his predecessor's tone to make it feel part of the same world. It just worked. Every element, from creature design to James Horner's Oscar-winning score to Weaver's Oscar-nominated performance, fizzed together like acid blood on metal.

the environment and the aliens "are coming out of the goddamn walls!" They quickly learn that they should have paid a lot more attention to their civilian advisor. The survivors must regroup, try to reestablish their connection with the ship, and realize that they are dealing with a threat that only Ripley understands.

It's a story about corporate malfeasance—the Weyland-Yutani Corp's determination to bring back living xenomorphs to the bio-weapons division leads directly to several deaths—and a story about taking personal responsibility. Michael Biehn, a last-minute substitute for James Remar as Hicks, gradually fades into the foreground in the male lead role, but it's Weaver's movie. Her performance here is even better than in *Alien*. She's a traumatized Cassandra warning of danger only to be ignored, and then a team player, and finally a lone warrior fighting to protect her surrogate daughter, the colony's sole survivor, Newt (Carrie Henn).

The film comes down to a desperate battle between Ripley and the alien queen, progenitor of those eggs from which the facehugger first sprang, battling it out for Newt and for survival. The appearance of that queen, the slow pan along a huge egg-belly to the nightmare body and crowned head of Stan Winston's iconic monster (based on

Left: The terrifying sounds made by the aliens were actually the shrieks of baboons that were altered in postproduction.

FACTS

ORIGINAL RELEASE DATE:
July 18, 1986 (U.S.); August 29, 1986 (UK)
RUN TIME: 148 minutes

DID YOU KNOW?
- The extended edition of the movie shows Ripley leaving behind a daughter when she went to work on the *Nostromo,* who died before she got home. This partly explains her bond with Newt.

FURTHER VIEWING
- *The Abyss* (1989)
  Cameron's next movie would bring together more benevolent aliens, Michael Biehn, and the deep sea exploration theme that has dominated much of his work since, in a story about an experimental submarine oil rig caught in a disastrous situation.

MUSCLE MEN & ACTION HEROES

If you wanted to be a movie star in the 1980s, one proven road to success was to hit the gym hard. Perhaps more than any other, this was a decade of bulging biceps and rippling pectorals. You could either practice martial arts for a lifetime or pump iron like there was no tomorrow—but either way, you could hope for Hollywood glory.

Above: Two of the 1980s' biggest action stars, Arnold Scwarzenegger and Carl Weathers, go face to face in *Predator*.

ARNOLD SCHWARZENEGGER

KEY 1980S MOVIES: *Predator*, *Commando*, *The Terminator*, *The Running Man*

STYLE: Bulging muscles, strangled Austrian accent, and a low-key sense of humor.

BEST 1980S ROLE: *The Terminator*, in which Schwarzenegger's robotic body language does all the talking.

AFTER THE 1980S: Arnie starred in a string of sequels and comedies, and—uh—became governor of California.

SYLVESTER STALLONE

KEY 1980S MOVIES: *First Blood*, *Rocky III*, *Cobra*, *Tango and Cash*

STYLE: Bulging muscles, rumbling New York accent, and surprising acting ability.

BEST 1980S ROLE: If Rocky is a 1970s character, then it has to be the increasingly macho Rambo.

AFTER THE 1980S: Stallone proved his acting talent in *Copland* and *Creed*, kept going with *Rambo* and *Rocky*, and created an action juggernaut with *The Expendables*.

BRUCE WILLIS

KEY 1980S MOVIES: *Blind Date*, *Die Hard*

STYLE: Sardonic, blue-collar everyman who is driven to action without looking for it.

BEST 1980S ROLE: He made only one 1980s action movie, but it was enough—*Die Hard*'s John McClane was made immortal.

AFTER THE 1980S: Willis played McClane another four times and proved adept in comedy (*Moonrise Kingdom*) and sci-fi (*The Fifth Element*) as well as action.

CHOW YUN FAT

KEY 1980S MOVIES: *The Killer*, *God of Killers*, *A Better Tomorrow*, *City on Fire*

STYLE: Ineffably cool, stylishly dressed, two-gun-toting killer.

BEST 1980S ROLE: Ah Jong in *The Killer* is his 1980s signature role, melding melancholy charm with a career as a ruthless assassin.

AFTER THE 1980S: He improved on *The Killer* in 1992's glorious *Hard Boiled*, and tackled wuxia in *Crouching Tiger, Hidden Dragon* with equal flair.

JACKIE CHAN

KEY 1980S MOVIES: *The Cannonball Run, Police Story, Dragons Forever*

STYLE: If Gene Kelly knew kung fu, it would look a lot like the impossibly fast, endlessly graceful Chan.

BEST 1980S ROLE: *Police Story*, which sees Chan really push the stunt envelope as a cop forced to clear his name when he's framed for corruption.

AFTER THE 1980S: Chan has broken nearly every bone in his body at some point in pursuit of martial arts perfection. He finally conquered Hollywood with *Shanghai Knights* and *Rush Hour*.

CHUCK NORRIS

KEY 1980S MOVIES: *Lone Wolf McQuade, The Delta Force, The Octagon, Missing in Action*

STYLE: Beard, all-American attitude, and a roundhouse kick to someone's head, every time.

BEST 1980S ROLE: McQuade, the Texas Ranger who takes down a drug kingpin with his martial arts know-how.

AFTER THE 1980S: Norris's most famous role in *Walker, Texas Ranger* came in the early 1990s. He also had a separate career as a best-selling author and created his own martial art, Chun Kuk Do.

CARL WEATHERS

KEY 1980S MOVIES: *Predator, Rocky IV, Action Jackson, Hurricane Smith*

STYLE: Tough, no-nonsense or slyly funny, but always extremely muscular.

BEST 1980S ROLE: His reprisal of Apollo Creed in *Rocky III*, when he became Rocky's trainer and friend, and tragic death in *Rocky IV* are standouts.

AFTER THE 1980S: Weathers showed a flair for comedy in *Happy Gilmore* and sent himself up on *Arrested Development*, where he played Carl Weathers, acting coach.

JEAN-CLAUDE VAN DAMME

KEY 1980S MOVIES: *Kickboxer, Cyborg, Bloodsport, No Retreat, No Surrender*

STYLE: High-kicking, splits-performing, Belgian-accented dynamo.

BEST 1980S ROLE: *Kickboxer*, his biggest hit, sees him at his best in a stripped-back plot about revenge and a martial arts tournament.

AFTER THE 1980S: His career stepped up a gear in the 1990s with *Hard Target* and *Universal Soldier*, and more recently he's taken to spoofing himself in titles such as *JCVD* and *Jean-Claude Van Johnson*.

Above: Sylvester Stallone's Rambo took some serious punishment over the years. With his shirt off, naturally.

STAND BY ME

1986

THE "COMING OF AGE" MOVIE IS SOMETIMES HACKNEYED, WITH CHARACTERS LEARNING VALUABLE LESSONS FROM WISE OLD MENTORS OR FALLING IN LOVE FOR THE FIRST TIME.

But *Stand by Me*, the film adaptation of Stephen King's novella *The Body*, is one of the most grounded and heartfelt examples of the genre ever made. That's despite the grisly premise: Four pre-teen boys go off into the woods in search of a corpse.

Gordie LaChance (Wil Wheaton) is twelve going on thirteen and at the end of his last summer before junior high school, in the small town of Castle Rock in the 1950s. He lost his brother Denny (John Cusack) a few months before and his parents aren't coping. With his best friend Chris (River Phoenix), slightly unhinged buddy Teddy (Corey Feldman), and sweet doofus Vern (Jerry O'Connell), he goes in search of the body of a local boy who went missing a few days before. The quartet hope to find the corpse

and become local heroes, but their journey along the railroad tracks and through the woods sets them on a different path.

Plot-wise, it is flimsy to the point of intangibility. Like *The Lord of the Rings*, it's basically a film of a long walk, although these achingly young men use the time to bicker and joke and begin to feel around the edges of what it means to be grown up instead of worrying about ancient jewelry. One minute, they are trying to figure out weighty questions of expectation and betrayal by adults; the next they're asking, "Mickey's a mouse, Donald's a duck, Pluto's a dog: what's Goofy?" Gordie has nightmares of his parents rejecting him, and Chris is tormented by the knowledge that his family's bad reputation

Below: *Stand by Me*'s four precocious leads: Wil Wheaton, River Phoenix, Corey Feldman, and Jerry O'Connell.

seems to have blighted his life before it starts. Teddy is a victim of abuse, and Vern, well, he means well. There is a remote threat in the person of Kiefer Sutherland's small-town bully Ace Merrill, but the boys' real problems are the parts of life they still can't figure out.

Key to the movie's success was the casting of the four boys, and director Rob Reiner did a stunning job there. "When you're casting twelve-year-old boys and thirteen-year-old boys, you really have to cast close to their personalities," he claimed. "You can't ask kids of that age to go very far away from who they are. They don't have the craft yet."

Sure enough, Wheaton was intelligent and awkward and sensitive; O'Connell was funny and kind of goofy; and Feldman was hyper but furiously unhappy underneath. From the earliest scenes, it's apparent that Chris is Gordie's protector as well as his friend. Phoenix was fifteen at the time, older than the other guys, and had to shave his legs to look as boyish as the rest. That extra maturity helps him play Chris, but it's Phoenix's natural empathy and extraordinary ability that does most of the work.

King incorporated elements of his own youth into the novella, using not only the kind of friendships he had at twelve but also the terrifying railway bridge and the leeches in the swimming hole. It was personal for Reiner, too, who identified with Gordie's attempts to win his parents' approval and escape his brother's shadow. At that time in his life, he still felt overshadowed by his father Carl Reiner's success, but he channeled those feelings, along with details of his own childhood, into the movie. He spent months with his stars, too, playing games with them that incidentally taught them to act naturally as a group. "If I'm any good as a director at all, it's because I was an actor," he claimed.

The movie gained an extra, unwanted resonance after Phoenix's tragically early death in 1994, at the age of only twenty-three. It's narrated by "the writer" (the adult Gordie, played by Reiner's childhood friend Richard Dreyfus), as he types his account of that summer. But his last lines are not spoken, only shown on-screen. Chris Chambers, we are told, did get out of Castle Rock, but he died in

adulthood when he tried to break up a fight between two strangers. Gordie writes, "Although I hadn't seen him in more than ten years, I know I'll miss him forever. I never had any friends later on like the ones I had when I was twelve. Jesus, does anyone?" Wheaton put it similarly twenty-five years after when he wrote of Phoenix, "When he was fifteen and I was thirteen, he was my friend. That's the person I knew, and that's the person I miss." Perhaps *Stand by Me* works as well as it does because, whatever the era in which it's set and whatever the object of the boys' quest, at its heart it's about something true.

Above: The film took on an even greater poignancy following the tragic death of River Phoenix in 1994.

ORIGINAL RELEASE DATE:
November 26, 1986 (U.S.); March 13, 1987 (UK)
RUN TIME: 87 minutes

DID YOU KNOW?
- This was Stephen King's favorite adaptation of his own work. He famously hated Stanley Kubrick's great version of *The Shining*, but despite the changes to his novella, this one struck home.

FURTHER VIEWING
- *The Shining* (1980)
  Stanley Kubrick's masterful adaptation of Stephen King's winter-set chiller remains the gold standard for psychological horrors and terrifying Jack Nicholson performances.

FACTS

FERRIS BUELLER'S DAY OFF

LET'S BE HONEST: FERRIS BUELLER IS PROBABLY A TERRIBLE PERSON.

He has no regard for anyone but himself, and he probably grew up to run some kind of Ponzi scheme. But on a high school level, there's something charming about his crazy schemes to get ahead.

"They bought it. Incredible. One of the worst performances of my career and they never doubted it for a second? How could I possibly be expected to handle school on a day like this?" That's the reaction of Matthew Broderick's Ferris when his parents accept his faked illness and agree that he should take the day off school, sparking serious suspicion from Dean of Students Edward R. Rooney (Jeffrey Jones). With the help of his hypochondriac friend Cameron (Alan Ruck), Ferris fakes the death of his girlfriend Sloane's (Mia Sara) grandmother to get her out of class as well, and the trio head to Chicago in Cameron's dad's priceless Ferrari 250 GT California (license plate: NRVOUS).

An elaborate web of deception supports the plan. Ferris has a Rube Goldberg–type device set up at home to make it sound as if he's lying in bed sick, as well as a carefully networked system of answering phone messages and calls to back up his web of lies. Back at school, a grassroots campaign to "Save Ferris" has begun, following rumors that he needs $50,000 for a kidney transplant—and the only person who knows what's really going on seems to be his sister Jeanie (Jennifer Grey), who just snarls at the universal support for her apparently charmed sibling. However, she's not the biggest danger. That man of order, Ed Rooney, goes on a quest to prove Ferris a liar, but he just doesn't think big enough.

Left: Matthew Broderick as Ferris. John Hughes cast him because he thought Broderick was charming; he would also have considered "Jimmy Stewart at 15."

He's looking for Ferris in local arcades (wrong Matthew Broderick movie—it would have worked on *WarGames'* David Lightman) and at home, while his quarry is having a grand old time in the Windy City.

Ferris and his friends pack an impossible amount into a day that stretches out infinitely. They climb the Sears Tower, visit the stock exchange, and con their way into lunch at a fancy restaurant by pretending to be "Abe Froman, the sausage king of Chicago." There's a baseball game to watch at Wrigley Field, and a tour of the Art Institute of Chicago. Ferris leads a parade through the city, a scene shot during a real event when 10,000 people answered a radio call offering them the chance to be in a John Hughes movie.

Despite the theoretically real-world setting, this is almost a magical realist fantasy, somehow capturing the feeling of that last week of school, when the usual rules cease to apply and everyone goes a little crazy. And the background detail, with the "Save Ferris" campaign growing from a few concerned students to a front-page event, or the joyride in the Ferrari with the *Star Wars* soundtrack, adds endless texture and comedy to the story. It's *Home Alone* on a citywide scale.

And it all culminates in Ferris's crazy dash through his neighbors' yards to beat his parents and his sister home. Somehow, all's well that ends well for everyone. Cameron gets the showdown with his distant father that he desperately needs in the movie's most emotional scene—maybe its only emotional scene. But that quick beat of a withdrawn, frightened boy finally standing up for himself is a belter. Meanwhile, Jeanie gets a sense of perspective, Ferris gets the car he dreamed of, and Rooney gets a humiliating, drawn-out comeuppance. Ferris's narration, direct to the audience and capped by a post-credit sting when such things were rare, has been much imitated (*Wayne's World, Deadpool*) but never bettered. And it all came together so smoothly. Writer-director John Hughes pitched the movie the day after he had the idea and wrote the script in a week, filling the story with his own passions (the Art Institute, the Beatles) and his own

ORIGINAL RELEASE DATE: June 11, 1986 (U.S.); February 13, 1987 (UK)
RUN TIME: 99 minutes

DID YOU KNOW?

- First Lady Barbara Bush quoted the movie at a 1990 graduation speech at Wellesley College. "Find the joy in life, because as Ferris Bueller said on his day off, 'Life moves pretty fast; if you don't stop and look around once in a while, you could miss it!'"

FURTHER VIEWING

- *Say Anything* (1989)
  John Cusack plays another teen with too much charisma for his own good, and makes one of the all-time great romantic gestures.

FACTS

high school memories. That's his school where Ferris picks Sloane up, and Ferris's bedroom is modeled on his teenage home.

However, Ferris, with his absolute confidence that everything will work out for him, is the teen everyone wishes they were. He's popular, smart (his grades are visible on Rooney's computer, and they're good), he's got a gorgeous girlfriend, and he has the world wrapped around his finger. He has everything he wants (OK—except a car) and, more important, he has a philosophy. "A person should not believe in an -ism, he should believe in himself." You can't say that Ferris doesn't live up to his own ideals.

Below: Broderick, Ruck, and Sara take the opportunity to browse through a museum.

"LIFE MOVES PRETTY FAST. IF YOU DON'T STOP AND LOOK AROUND ONCE IN A WHILE, YOU COULD MISS IT."

Ferris Bueller (Matthew Broderick), *FERRIS BUELLER'S DAY OFF*

CROCODILE DUNDEE

1986

IN 1985, AUSTRALIAN STAR PAUL HOGAN HAD A PROBLEM.

He was hugely successful, with television comedy specials aired around the world and a career in advertising that made him the face of not only Fosters' lager but, through his work for the tourist board, Australia itself (he popularized the "shrimp on the barbie" phrase). However, television kept demanding more, with U.S. networks wanting another twenty-six half-hour shows, but preferring fifty-two, if he could manage it, ideally yesterday. It had taken Hogan and his team four years to produce the previous twenty-six, after all. So Hogan came up with a better idea—he'd make a movie. But not just any movie: he'd make a crowd-pleasing, fish-out-of-water blockbuster unlike anything his country's cinema had ever produced.

What he came up with was the story of American journalist Sue Charlton (Linda Kozlowski), who visits the Australian outback to chase the spectacular story of a fisherman who had his leg bitten off by a crocodile but crawled home to tell the tale. She soon learns that this was an exaggerated version of the story of Mick "Crocodile" Dundee (Hogan), a larger-than-life bushman with an impish sense of humor. He takes her on a guided tour into the wilderness to see where he was attacked, and in return she takes him back home to New York City as an attraction grows between them.

It's a threadbare plot, less a coherent movie with arc and themes and more an excuse for a series of sketches as Mick experiences big city life. He figures that with "seven million people all wantin' to live together . . . New York must be the friendliest place on Earth." The gap between his quasi-logic and reality is gaping, but Mick's genial ignorance turns out to be a shield as he, for example, sees a man snorting cocaine, assumes it's cold medication, and empties his entire stash into some hot water to

Below: The original poster for the film. Paul Hogan was already a celebrity worldwide for his TV comedy specials, and the film aimed to cash in on that fame.

create a nice steam treatment. Mick's the kind of guy who gets into conversation with two friendly sex workers and, when rudely interrupted by their pimp, knocks him out and apologizes to the ladies for the man's bad language. He's a gentleman, in other words—just an unconventional one.

The movie, directed by Hogan's longtime collaborator Peter Faiman, was very much of its time in its sexual, LGBT, and race politics. Mick gropes a trans-woman to establish her genitalia and asks an African American limo driver what "tribe" he belongs to, being a "black fella." Despite that, his air of well-meaning cluelessness somewhat blunts the offensiveness and makes this film less jarring to revisit than some of its contemporaries. The movie at least acknowledges that many Indigenous Australians live in cities, and pokes fun at Sue's assumption that they must be superstitious rather than poking fun at their actual beliefs. They're portrayed at least as positively as the lead, who is flummoxed by an escalator. Mick's total political disengagement, however, is unappealing; his claim that disputes over Australian land ownership are "like two fleas arguing over the dog" feels disingenuous coming from a white man, given Australia's history.

The love story is patchy. Sue is played as an independent woman, which is good, but she's working for her dad and her boyfriend, which undercuts her success. You can see her attraction to Mick's roguish ways, but she doesn't consistently show a preference for him over her obviously unsatisfying yuppie boyfriend Richard (Mark Blum), so it's arguable whether that iconic subway ending is earned, as Sue declares her love via two blue-collar intermediaries along a crowded platform.

And yet, Mick Dundee has an old-world appeal to his behavior, a throwback to a mythical time when men were honorable and true. "Why do you always make me feel like Jane in a Tarzan comic?" says Sue after the iconic scene where Mick responds to a would-be mugger with "That's not a knife; *that's* a knife" and brandishes his machete. She's right: There are deliberate echoes of Tarzan here, and a hint of Frank Capra's *Mr. Deeds Goes to Town*. But Mick's his own fella, a self-created Australian myth for all his countrymen to live up to.

The movie did exactly what Hogan hoped. It was a massive hit worldwide, and incidentally provided a huge boost for Australian tourism, thanks to the film's glorious depiction of Kakadu National Park. If it was cynically conceived and a little backward in its execution, it is never malicious, and its good heart carries it through where other big, commercial movies have fallen into disgrace. That's got to be worth another shrimp or two on the barbie.

Above: The famous "That's not a knife" scene, wherein a mugger with a small flick knife gets rather more than he bargained for from his latest victim.

ORIGINAL RELEASE DATE:
September 26, 1986 (U.S.); December 12, 1986 (UK)
RUN TIME: 97 minutes

DID YOU KNOW?
◆ Paul Hogan first broke into entertainment on a talent show called *New Faces*, where he poked fun at the (consistently harsh) judges and turned the audience against them.

FURTHER VIEWING
◆ *Coming to America* (1988)
Skip the disappointing *Dundee* sequels and watch another fish-out-of-water story as Eddie Murphy plays an African prince looking for his ideal woman in—where else?—the New York borough of Queens.

FACTS

HIGHLANDER

IT'S A CULT CLASSIC, BUT EVEN DIE-HARD FANS CANNOT DENY THAT *HIGHLANDER* IS ALSO ONE OF THE WEIRDEST MOVIES OF THE 1980S.

A heavily accented Frenchman plays a medieval, immortal Scottish warrior. A Scotsman, one who doesn't bother with fripperies such as accents, brings us the Egyptian-born, Spanish-ennobled, and Japanese-equipped fighter who trains him. And an elegant premise—"There can be only one"—is entirely unwound by the five sequels, two spin-off live-action shows, and three animations that followed.

Christopher Lambert is the glowering Connor MacLeod, the Scotsman who discovers, after being stabbed through the heart during a sixteenth-century clan war, that he is an Immortal. The only way to kill one of these beings is by beheading, and, with each duel to the death, the survivor gains a portion of "the Quickening," a state of godlike knowledge and power. Or something—it's not entirely clear. But amid superstition and suspicion, poor young Connor is rejected by his people, so he has to leave and find a new life elsewhere in the Highlands and a new love, Heather (Beatie Edney). However, Immortals can sense one another, so Sean Connery's Ramírez seeks him out and becomes the mentor who explains the rules and trains Connor in the techniques needed to survive centuries of one-on-one mortal combat. Lurking on the sidelines is Clancy Brown as the Kurgan, earning his place in the cult movie pantheon as "perfect warrior," an unrepentantly dark force who stands between Connor and godhood or, indeed, survival.

Our guide to this world is Brenda Wyatt (Roxanne Hart), a contemporary New York police pathologist who moonlights as a historical metallurgist. After investigating the scene of Connor's latest (and frankly shambolic) duel in a wrestling arena parking lot, she wants to know why there's a piece of a sword

Left: Christopher Lambert strikes a heroic pose as immortal Scotsman Connor MacLeod.

that shouldn't exist in the body of his latest opponent. Flashbacks explain the rest, although Connor does offer an impressive practical demonstration of his immortality when he forces her to stab him through the chest. This, it emerges, is his way of flirting.

There is an inevitability and a pulse to this movie that manages to overcome its frequent silliness, and a surprising amount of emotion as Connor watches his first love grow old and die while he remains eternally young. Being immortal isn't all about trying out exciting new haircuts and picking up a French accent; it's also about endless vigilance in case one of your own kind decides to separate your head from your neck. Even in rainy, overstylized 1980s New York, Connor has to make sure that his overcoats are sufficiently baggy to hide a sword, so he is always ready for an impromptu duel to the death.

However fun the story, the casting is still weird. Mulcahy saw a photo of Lambert in the Tarzan film *Greystoke* and immediately decided that he had found his man. It was only later that he learned the actor spoke broken English with a noticeable French burr, and while the game Lambert trained four hours a day for months to improve his English, he never entirely sounded either Scottish or, in deference to his adopted homeland, American. At least he had the comfort of knowing his was not the weakest accent in the cast. Connery apparently worked with a dialogue coach to help establish a Spanish voice, but his natural brogue is far too strong to allow for any conditioning.

Still, who's to say how medieval Scots actually spoke? Perhaps they all sounded French. The real point of *Highlander* is Connor's eternal quest to become a real boy and rejoin the human race; actor Nick Offerman described this as "the greatest film about becoming a man that I've ever seen." This story paints Connor's situation as a tragedy rather than a gift; he's more wandering Jew than gifted superhero. He can't be killed, but he still feels pain and worse; he feels the sting of rejection by his community and the long-ago death of his wife, and so many lesser losses since.

Still, at least Connor gets to hang out with Sean Connery and admire his doublet, and he has a

chance to behead people with a sword. By the time that he finally faces his nemesis, the Kurgan, with lightning flashing around them, the soul of the whole world at stake, and that Queen soundtrack in the air, it's impossible not to be at least a little swept up. Despite its flaws, this movie will quicken the pulse.

ORIGINAL RELEASE DATE: March 7, 1986 (U.S.); August 29, 1986 (UK)
RUN TIME: 111 minutes

DID YOU KNOW?
- In preparation for the movie, Lambert spent four hours a day training with Bob Anderson, the veteran fencer who choreographed fights in *Star Wars* and *The Princess Bride*.

FURTHER VIEWING
- *The Untouchables* (1987)
  Connery's best performance in the 1980s was in Brian De Palma's superstylish, superquotable gangster movie ("They pull a knife, you pull a gun . . . ") opposite Kevin Costner and Robert De Niro. It deservedly landed him an Oscar.

FACTS

Below: MacLeod is tutored in the ways of the Immortals by Ramírez (Sean Connery), who's thousands of years old and widely traveled.

LABYRINTH

1986

THE 1980S IS GENERALLY REGARDED AS A BAD DECADE FOR FANTASY—UNSURPRISINGLY—GIVEN DISAPPOINTMENTS SUCH AS *KRULL, BEASTMASTER,* AND *HAWK THE SLAYER.*

But there were bright spots. *Willow* is an immense amount of fun, and *Ladyhawke* has some wildly romantic moments. The decade's best high fantasies, however, both involved puppets. Jim Henson quietly made two classics with *The Dark Crystal* and this uneasy blend of fairy-tale tropes. In *Labyrinth*, the princess is also the intrepid hero on a quest to rescue someone; the villain is dangerously close to being a love interest, and the supporting cast has some of the most charming characters ever created, because most of them are puppets.

The story starts with Jennifer Connelly's rebellious, dreamy Sarah sulking because she's been ordered to babysit for her brother Toby instead of dancing about in the local park, pretending to be a fairy princess. This is a teenager ahead of her time,

a proper millennial who likes flower crowns and doesn't worry too much about what society thinks of her. But then she wishes that the goblins she dreams of would come and take the crying baby away, and, when her wish is granted, she's horrified. She sets out to rescue Toby from Goblin King Jareth (David Bowie), with the help—and sometimes hindrance—of a gang of fantastical creatures.

It's a complicated movie, because Sarah is not a simple heroine, and the Goblin King is not a straightforward monster. Sarah caused her own problems, although she has some extenuating circumstances. She's still grieving for her mother, adjusting uneasily to her new stepmother, and burying herself in books instead of trying to establish a new family normality. But as a consequence of her

fit of rage, she must solve riddles, face dangerous obstacles, and face losing her heart (and soul?) to the Goblin King before she can get home and work things out.

The film began development soon after *The Dark Crystal* was finished, with designer Brian Froud and Jim Henson deciding to work together again but on a lighter story. Froud had the idea of a baby surrounded by goblins and the script went from there, although it went through many, many drafts before reaching the filmed version. Monty Python's Terry Jones did the majority of the work, but there were contributions from Henson, producer George Lucas, Laura Phillips, and comedy legend Elaine May. Bowie was first asked to get involved in 1983 and contributed his thoughts on many versions of the story until formally signing on in 1985, a few months before shooting began. Candidates for the role of Sarah included Jane Krakowski (*30 Rock*), Yasmine Bleeth (*Baywatch*), and Helena Bonham Carter before Connelly landed it at the age of fourteen, balanced precisely between childhood and adulthood.

Connelly's acting was not, at this point, quite up to the Oscar-winning standard she would reach as an adult, and she's not helped by the fact that Sarah is a huge drama queen who declaims most of the lines in her first scenes instead of talking like a normal person. But she gets visibly more comfortable as the movie progresses, and she's utterly convincing when she's interacting with puppets. Her personal Scooby Gang are the cowardly Hoggle (Shari Weiser/Brian Henson), towering rock enthusiast Ludo (Ron Mueck), and the valiant fox terrier, knight in shining armor Sir Didymus (David Shaughnessy) on his noble English sheepdog steed, and they all loosen things up immeasurably.

Of course, it helped to have Bowie as the male lead. Few pop stars of any era could dance around in breeches that tight, in a shirt that frilly, with hair that large, and emerge with their dignity intact—yet he does, and his music gives the film a much-needed edge. He's surrounded by goblins (he even kicks one mid-dance number) and yet you never doubt that he fits in among them, nor that there is a real danger that he could win Sarah's affections and entice her to stay with him in the labyrinth.

There is a strong suggestion that the entire adventure is taking place inside Sarah's head. The characters are based on her toys, the Goblin King is a statue on her dressing table, and her gorgeous, magical ball gown is based on her music box. At the end of the movie, Sarah packs away some of these things, the most obvious mementos of her mother, and that signals real growth. But her capacity for fantasy remains. Before the credits roll, she has called up her monster friends and they dance around her bedroom, because sometimes you need a little fantasy to make the real world bearable.

Left: Sarah (Jennifer Connelly) in her fantastical ball gown finery for the dream (or is it?) sequence where she fights Jareth's attempts to seduce her to his side.

ORIGINAL RELEASE DATE: June 27, 1986 (U.S.); December 2, 1986 (UK)
RUN TIME: 98 minutes

DID YOU KNOW?

◆ The director of puppet movement on this film and *The Dark Crystal* was Cheryl McFadden—better known as Gates McFadden, aka Dr. Beverly Crusher in *Star Trek: The Next Generation*.

FURTHER VIEWING

◆ *The Dark Crystal* (1982)
Henson's other wild fantasy movie is the story of two small elves, or Gelflings, who try to save their world by restoring a missing shard to a Dark Crystal. It's a surprisingly dark story involving death, mind control, and some of the scariest villains ever seen in a children's movie.

FACTS

1987 HIGHLIGHTS

With *Moonstruck* and *The Witches of Eastwick*, Cher became a major movie star in 1987, while the year's biggest film was directed by Mr. Spock himself, Leonard Nimoy. Glenn Close boiled Michael Douglas's bunny in *Fatal Attraction*, while Timothy Dalton took over as James Bond for *The Living Daylights*.

HIGHEST-GROSSING FILMS (U.S.)

1. *Three Men and a Baby*	Disney	$167,780,960
2. *Fatal Attraction*	Paramount	$156,645,693
3. *Beverly Hills Cop II*	Paramount	$153,665,036
4. *Good Morning, Vietnam*	Disney	$123,922,370
5. *Moonstruck*	Metro-Goldwyn-Mayer	$80,640,528
6. *The Untouchables*	Paramount	$76,270,454
7. *The Secret of My Success*	Universal	$66,995,000
8. *Stakeout*	Disney	$65,673,23
9. *Lethal Weapon*	Warner Bros.	$65,207,127
10. *The Witches of Eastwick*	Warner Bros.	$63,766,510

AT THE GOLDEN GLOBES

Best Picture (Drama)	*The Last Emperor*
Best Picture (Comedy/Musical)	*Hope and Glory*
Best Director	Bernardo Bertolucci, *The Last Emperor*
Best Actor (Drama)	Michael Douglas, *Wall Street*
Best Actor (Comedy/Musical)	Robin Williams, *Good Morning, Vietnam*
Best Actress (Drama)	Sally Kirkland, *Anna*
Best Actress (Comedy/Musical)	Cher, *Moonstruck*

CANNES FILM FESTIVAL

Palme d'Or winner
Under the Sun of Satan, Maurice Pialat

NOTABLE DEATHS

Danny Kaye, March 3	Actor, *White Christmas* and *The Court Jester*
Rita Hayworth, May 14	Actor, *Gilda* and *The Loves of Carmen*
Fred Astaire, June 22	Actor, *Top Hat* and *Shall We Dance*
Jackie Gleason, June 24	Actor and comedian, *The Hustler* and *The Honeymooners*
John Huston, August 28	Director, *The African Queen* and *Key Largo*
Lee Marvin, August 29	Actor, *The Dirty Dozen* and *The Man Who Shot Liberty Valance*

AT THE OSCARS

Best Picture	*The Last Emperor*
Best Director	Bernardo Bertolucci, *The Last Emperor*
Best Actor	Michael Douglas, *Wall Street*
Best Actress	Cher, *Moonstruck*

THIS YEAR'S BIG OSCARS INJUSTICE

Sean Connery's great in *The Untouchables*, but Denzel Washington should probably have taken his first Oscar this year as Best Supporting Actor for *Cry Freedom*.

FUTURE MOVIE STAR BIRTHS

February 9: Michael B. Jordan, *Creed* and *Black Panther*
February 21: Ellen Page, *Juno* and *Hard Candy*
July 27: Mara Wilson, *Mrs. Doubtfire* and *Miracle on 34th Street*
September 22: Tom Felton, *Harry Potter* series and *Rise of the Planet of the Apes*
October 18: Zac Efron, *Hairspray* and *The Greatest Showman*

NOTABLE FILM DEBUTS

Jason Bateman, *Teen Wolf Too*
Sandra Bullock, *Hangmen*
George Clooney, *Return to Horror High*
Gong Li, *Red Sorghum*
Brad Pitt, *No Man's Land*
Robin Wright, *The Princess Bride*

WALL STREET

1987

HANG OUT WITH STOCKBROKERS NOW, AND YOU WILL STILL HEAR SOME CLAIM THAT "GREED IS GOOD" OR "LUNCH IS FOR WIMPS."

These lines, from Oliver Stone's *Wall Street*, have been adopted by the very men they were meant to skewer, suggesting that Stone made one fatal error in his Oscar-winning movie. He made his bad guy too charismatic.

It's meant to be the story of Bud Fox (Charlie Sheen), a young wannabe plugging away in a minor investment house, cold-calling prospective stock buyers. Bud has big dreams and forces his way into the orbit of Gordon Gekko (Michael Douglas), a Wall Street investor who has the power to make or break Bud's career. The younger man brings a piece of inside information that could make them both a

fortune, but Gekko leads him further and further onto questionable ground as useful intelligence becomes true insider trading. They're both riding high on the results, with Gekko providing Bud with hookers, entry to private clubs, and even the interior decorator who becomes his girlfriend, Darien Taylor (Daryl Hannah). There's a precipitous fall to come, as Bud overreaches and Gekko's friendship turns out to be unreliable. But in the end, the character everyone remembers is Gordon Gekko, and they remember his success rather than his comeuppance.

This is a portrait of high finance that was made as a period piece. Shot in 1987, it was set in 1985, a

Above: Charlie Sheen and Daryl Hannah take a break from the ruthless world of the New York Stock Exchange.

Right: Gekko's cigar-chomping, larger-than-life ways saw him adopted as something of a mascot by Wall Street traders, who still quote his "Greed is good" mantra.

tiny time jump that helped Wall Street to distance itself from Gekko's behavior and persuade the New York Stock Exchange to give Stone access to the floor (Stone also credited the Exchange's Vietnam veterans and *Platoon* fans for getting him access). Michael Douglas modeled his portrayal of Gekko partly on Donald Trump, with that bouffant hair and extravagant lifestyle (Trump loved the comparison), and based his "Greed is good" speech on a real speech by corporate raider Ivan Boesky. However, the movie has become more relevant since its release, somehow more timely than its own 2010 sequel. The rapacious greed, and the perception that the markets are a game, has continued since the 1980s, through the tech bubble and the 2008 financial crash.

The movie's success at the box office and Academy Awards is testament to Douglas's scene-stealing performance and Stone's macho, broad-strokes direction. The story was close to Stone's heart—his father had been the kind of honorable trader played by Hal Holbrook, and the director himself makes a fleeting cameo—and you can see it in the detail, such as the stock slips and the real locations (there are no studio scenes). It's also there in the scathing portrayal of the rich, from Darien's awful interior design and Gekko's horrible art collection to Bud's half-hearted plea "Who am I?" at the height of his success, a dip into self-awareness that lasts about half a second. Bud's tears as he's arrested show the weakness under his bravado, like the blackout on Gekko when he agrees to sell his shares low and write off tens of millions of dollars.

Stone saw this very much as a companion piece to *Platoon*, saying, "They can take your life in Vietnam; they can take your soul on Wall Street." But the director didn't devote as much time to the good guy in this story. In *Platoon*, the tug of love between good mentor (Willem Dafoe) and bad influence (Tom Berenger) feels almost equal. But after a promising first scene here, Martin Sheen's good dad is sidelined, saddled with some of the most on-the-nose dialogue in movie history, and the movie's ostensible villain runs the table. Many viewers also missed the movie's moral and decided that Gekko

wasn't such a bad guy. "Michael, in the supporting role, has simply stolen the picture from my hero," Stone said, discussing how the movie backfired. "Charlie didn't even get an Oscar nomination. [Brokers] all dismissed Charlie as a schmuck. Their attitude was, 'What is Michael Douglas doing that is so wrong?'"

It's also a movie with barely a single decent female character, and several terrible ones. But what the movie does, it does well. It communicates the all-or-nothing mentality of high finance, the complete divorce of money from production, and the misanthropy of finance's titans. Everything Gekko says, in his penultimate confrontation with Bud ("I create nothing. I own."), is still true, perhaps more than it ever was. "You're not naive enough to think we're living in a democracy, are you, Buddy? It's the free market, and you're part of it." Broad morality play aside, *Wall Street* is scary because it's accurate.

ORIGINAL RELEASE DATE: December 11, 1987 (U.S.); April 29, 1988 (UK)
RUN TIME: 126 minutes

DID YOU KNOW?

- One of the movie's financial consultants, Kenneth Lipper, ordered Charlie Sheen to invest $15,000 of his own money to experience what it felt like to lose money on the stock market. Alas, he made a four-figure profit.

FURTHER VIEWING

- *Scarface* (1983)
  If you enjoy stories about wrongdoing in pursuit of the American dream, try Brian De Palma's no-holds-barred account of Tony Montana's (Al Pacino) rise to power in the Miami drug trade.

FACTS

"GREED IS GOOD."

Gordon Gekko (Michael Douglas), *WALL STREET*

PREDATOR

THE 1980S WAS A DECADE OF BIG MUSCLES, AND NO MOVIE HAS BIGGER, SWEATIER, MORE BULGING ONES THAN *PREDATOR*.

It's as if someone wondered, "What if Rambo had bros?" and came to the logical conclusion that no power on Earth could stand against him. So screenwriters Jim and John Thomas and director John McTiernan conceived an alien as a challenge, cast Arnold Schwarzenegger at the peak of his size in the lead, and made an action-sci-fi-horror that is a glorious, brawny blast.

The script is as muscular as the characters, with relationships established via arm wrestling, tobacco chewing, and dirty jokes. Shane Black, then the hot screenwriter in town after *Lethal Weapon* (see page 126) refused to polish this script when the studio asked him (he thought it was already perfect) but

took a role as Hawkins just to see how it went down. There was plenty of drama to entertain him. The set was famously troubled: most of the cast and crew got stomach bugs from the water on the Mexican location, and the cast's gym schedules were all-consuming. Not to mention the fact that the entire end of the movie had to be reshot with a new Predator after the original martial arts–heavy concept (worn by Jean-Claude Van Damme) was dumped in favor of Stan Winston's mandibled monster.

Our first glimpse of Schwarzenegger's Major "Dutch" Schaefer comes when he lights his cigar in the shadows inside a helicopter, the flame revealing his massive profile. But Dutch is not exactly as gung ho as his mountainous appearance suggests. He initially objects to the mission on the basis that "we're a rescue team, not assassins," and when reminded of the team's exploits in Afghanistan, he squelches any triumphalism with "I'm trying to forget it." It makes sense for the leader of this gang to be the voice of wisdom, kind of, and it establishes Dutch as the father figure heading an unlikely blood brotherhood. Then there's Jesse Ventura's blithely confident Blaine and his BFF Mac (Bill Duke), the intellectual Poncho (Richard Chaves) and nervy Hawkins, Carl Weathers's CIA operative Dillon, Sonny Landham's spiritual scout Bill, and enemy prisoner Anna (Elpidia Carrillo). It's a small enough gang for each to be distinctive, but big enough to satisfy the need for regular, spectacular deaths.

Yet despite the confidence of these hulking macho men, this movie is a jangling nerve, a steady exercise in paranoia and creeping flesh. All but the first ten minutes take place in enemy territory, and it's not the enemy our elite team expected to fight. So

Left: Stan Winston's Predator design in all its dreadlocked, mandibled glory. No wonder it prefers to wear a mask.

there's fear of a Central American native emerging from the jungle (more shades of Vietnam) linked to the terror of a threat that is brutal, technologically superior, and largely unfathomable. Kevin Peter Hall, the basketball player who donned the final suit, compared his moves to those of a medieval knight, and there's a sense of ritual about the Predator's hunting—skinning his captives just as early settlers in the Americas scalped Native Americans—that is all the more terrifying for being so, well, alien (in an unlikely turn, Hall played the pacifist Bigfoot in *Harry and the Hendersons* the same year). It's also insanely cool. We'd never seen digital camouflage like this before, nor the Predator's heat vision.

Predator is a movie so macho that it almost comes back out the other side into completely camp. "I ain't got time to bleed," says Blaine, who's also carrying "Ol' Painless," a gun designed to be bolted to a helicopter, which the moviemakers picked because it looks cooler than any real handheld weapon. Meanwhile, Dutch tells the man he just impaled to a wall to "stick around" with immense satisfaction. And, of course, it comes down to a struggle *mano a mano* between the Earth's mightiest soldier and the alien adventurer. Dutch goes back to basics, hauling logs, setting traps, and covering himself in dirt to escape the alien's notice, because despite their love

of shiny technology, the winner in American movies is usually the guy with the low-tech, homemade solution (see also *Rocky IV*, *Star Wars*, *Avatar*).

However, the Predator has the last laugh, literally, and triggers a self-destruct that releases a small mushroom cloud while Dutch races to safety. Presumably, it's not a real nuke, because as we all learned from Schwarzenegger's *True Lies*, the minimum safe distance is twelve miles and Dutch clearly can't run that far, that fast. Then again, how could an action movie this thick with sinew end except with the Bomb? Nothing else would slow these guys down.

ORIGINAL RELEASE DATE: June 12, 1987 (U.S.); January 1, 1988 (UK)
RUN TIME: 102 minutes

DID YOU KNOW?

- Sometimes the movie's main unit had to stop shooting, because the second unit explosions were so big they diffused the light of the sun in the area.

FURTHER VIEWING

- *Commando* (1985)
  Schwarzenegger's preposterous action classic is stuffed to the gills with ludicrous kiss-off lines ("Let off some steam, Bennett").

FACTS

Below: Dutch (Arnold Schwarzenegger), Dillon (Carl Weathers), and Mac (Bill Duke) face a tense situation.

LETHAL WEAPON

1987

THERE WERE BUDDY COP MOVIES BEFORE *LETHAL WEAPON*, BUT SOMEHOW THIS FILM FEELS LIKE THE FIRST OF ITS KIND.

Its model—mismatched partners, giant action scenes, and endless quippery—became ubiquitous, overshadowing all that had gone before. It almost entirely displaced the lone-wolf stories of the 1970s (*Serpico*, *The French Connection*), thanks to the chemistry of its leads, the light touch of its director, and one of the great action scripts.

It began with the screenplay, a brash calling card from new talent Shane Black. The script's humor, scale, and macho appeal caught the eye of producer Joel Silver, already a big name thanks to *Commando*, *Weird Science*, and *48 Hrs*. He brought Richard Donner on board, and the pair took Black's work and ran with it.

The movie opens in a way that's still shocking. After a cheerful rendition of "Jingle Bell Rock" and a pan across nighttime Los Angeles, a beautiful, scantily clad girl snorts drugs and throws herself off a balcony. Cut to LAPD Detective Roger Murtaugh (Danny Glover), sitting morose in the bath before his family bursts in to celebrate his fiftieth birthday. Across town, in a beachfront trailer home, Mel Gibson's magnificently mulleted Martin Riggs is also naked, stumbling drunk out of bed to his first beer of the day. Murtaugh learns that the dead girl is the daughter of an old Vietnam buddy, and that Riggs is his new partner, and we're off to the races. Murtaugh's too old for this stuff, and Riggs is secretly hoping that some friendly bullet will put him out of his misery following his wife's death, but, first, both have to solve the girl's murder.

It's the chemistry between Glover and Gibson that's key, the unlikely pair forming a bromance that transforms, over the film's three sequels, into something like true love. The steadiness and depth of their relationship in later movies sometimes blunts the memory of how hard-earned it is here. From a disastrous first meeting, they bicker incessantly until they bond over their first dead bad guy. Murtaugh gives Riggs the stability and family life that he lost when his wife died; Riggs gives Murtaugh the sense of fearlessness that makes him feel young again. They complete one another.

Like Indiana Jones (page 32), Riggs and Murtaugh fail at least as often as they succeed, such as in their disastrous attempt to rescue Murtaugh's hostage daughter Rianne (Traci Wolfe). But they get it right when it counts, even if that means chasing a car down an L.A. freeway on foot, bare-chested. Which of course it does, because this movie is steeped in machismo. Of course, the bad guy (Gary Busey), once cornered, must be defeated hand to hand, despite already being held at gunpoint. And, of course, he can't accept defeat and must be shot dead anyway. It's that kind of movie—manly pride demands nothing less.

This was a star-making role for Mel Gibson, who gives it a touch of John Wayne style in lines such as "You do this my way. You shoot, you shoot to kill, get as many of them as you can." *Mad Max* may have been his breakthrough for moviemakers, but the wider audience, for the most part, first encountered him here. It's at least partly love for the tragic, valiant Martin Riggs that has kept the second chances coming when Gibson himself behaved appallingly in real life. Glover should have had just as big a career boost; blame the narrower options for black actors in the 1980s.

The film is casually, repeatedly sexist, from the opening piece of titillation to the utter contempt for well-meaning (and largely correct) departmental psychiatrist Stephanie Woods (Mary Ellen Trainor). But it's also funny and generally anarchic ("I've seen this place on lifestyles of the rich and shameless"), which helps blunt the offensiveness. Still, machismo and all, the movie is a perfect distillation of the 1980s. There's a cell phone the size of a lunch box, action scenes that would see any real police officer immediately suspended, and that mullet. This is both the quintessential buddy cop movie and nothing of

the kind. Really, they're only buddies in the last act, and barely cops at all in any realistic sense. At heart, this is a cowboy fantasy, an adolescent boy's adventure with a budget for explosions. But that sizzling chemistry and sense of pace make that fantasy endlessly appealing.

Opposite: Martin Riggs (Mel Gibson) squares up to take his shot, despite the weight of his huge mullet.

Above: Riggs and Murtaugh (Danny Glover) face off. Who'd have thought these two were made for each other?

ORIGINAL RELEASE DATE: March 6, 1987 (U.S.); August 28, 1987 (UK)
RUN TIME: 109 minutes

DID YOU KNOW?
- Darlene Love, who plays Trish Murtaugh, is best known as a singer. She recorded "Christmas Time (Baby Please Come Home)," a Christmas classic that fits this movie's seasonal setting perfectly.

FURTHER VIEWING
- *48 Hrs* (1982)
  Almost entirely overshadowed by *Lethal Weapon*, this hit Nick Nolte/Eddie Murphy buddy movie preceded it by five years. It's notable for similar humor, as well as for being Eddie Murphy's screen debut and first Golden Globe nomination.

FACTS

FATAL ATTRACTION

1987

"DIDN'T YOU SEE *FATAL ATTRACTION*?" ASKS TOM HANKS'S SAM IN *SLEEPLESS IN SEATTLE*. IT'S A RHETORICAL QUESTION—ALMOST EVERY MAN IN AMERICA SAW IT, AND IT FREAKED THEM ALL OUT.

There had been other 1980s erotic thrillers before Adrian Lyne's *Fatal Attraction*—*Body Heat*; *9½ Weeks* (also by Lyne); *Jagged Edge*—but this six-time Oscar nominee was the most successful and, as Tom Hanks's character later suggested, by far the most influential. This affair gone horribly wrong has passed into legend, and the insult "bunny boiler" is familiar even to people who never saw it.

Fatal Attraction is based on a short film by James Dearden, who also wrote this screenplay (and later turned it into a play). He set out to write a "minimalist" idea, something cheap to shoot, and came up with a man who has an affair while his wife is away for the weekend, only to find that his lover isn't ready to drop the attachment on Monday morning. Producers Stanley Jaffe and Sherry Lansing asked him to expand the idea, so he moved the setting to New York and came up with new and disturbing ways to turn the screws on his antihero.

That's how we get Michael Douglas's Dan Gallagher. He has a beautiful wife, Beth (Anne Archer), a tiny daughter, Ellen, and a dog when he meets Alex Forest (Glenn Close). She knows he is married but still has an eye for him. While Beth and Ellen are out of town, Dan and Alex go out for dinner. Dan babbles, nervous, and Alex seems in control.

Above: Along with *Wall Street*, *Fatal Attraction* cemented Michael Douglas as one of the most bankable stars of 1987.

Right: Glenn Close earned an Academy Award nomination for her performance, which swerved between violent and calculated.

But he responds quickly to her advances and soon they are all over each other on the kitchen counter. They go dancing, back to her place, and get busy in the elevator. She's insatiable, and when he goes back to his family, she can't let go.

She argues as he tries to leave. He claims, "The opportunity was there and we took it . . . you knew the rules." "What rules?" she replies. She runs hot and cold; angry, conciliatory, tearful, clawing at him. She cuts her wrists in a final attempt to stop him from leaving. The next time she sees him, it's all smiles and apologies, but then she finds him again, tells him she's pregnant, and really begins to pressure him to "acknowledge your responsibilities." It gets to the point when every ring of the phone triggers near panic and Alex seems to stalk Dan around every corner.

Soon the relationship turns violent. He breaks into her apartment; she attacks his car, stews his daughter's pet rabbit, and even takes the girl for an afternoon at an amusement park. He tries to choke her to death; she tries to stab him. Finally, she attacks Beth in his home and is killed—first nearly drowned by Dan, then shot in the chest by Beth.

Fights have raged for years about whether the movie is antifeminist, because it pits a career woman against a homemaker and the former loses conclusively. All the attention is generally focused on the unhappy Alex and her increasingly desperate attempts to entice Dan back into her bed ("I'm not going to be ignored, Dan"), but what's much less talked about are Dan's failings. There are traces of nervousness at the start of his affair, but he throws himself into it with little hesitation or guilt. The visible regret comes only when Alex threatens his marriage and forces him to face the consequences of his actions. Maybe this should be read less as an indictment of any particular type of woman and more of faithless men.

The movie's original ending had Alex kill herself in an attempt to frame Dan, but the more violent finish came after test audiences demanded a more emphatic finale. Close fought it, believing it out of character, but it follows the escalating path of Dan and Alex's struggle to a climax that is almost logical. If

ORIGINAL RELEASE DATE:
September 18, 1987 (U.S.); February 15, 1988 (UK)
RUN TIME: 114 minutes

DID YOU KNOW?

◆ Dan's boss, Arthur, is played by Fred Gwynne, best known for his role as Hermann Munster on *The Munsters*.

FURTHER VIEWING

◆ *Dangerous Liaisons* (1988)
See Glenn Close in a sexy, dangerous, but far-more-controlled role in Stephen Frears's adaptation of the classic French story; she plays the amoral schemer who plays with her lovers' lives.

FACTS

there's a cop-out, it comes later, when the police just drop the issue of the dead woman in the Gallaghers' bathroom and the couple hug, the camera panning in on their family portrait. It's a too-happy ending for what's gone on before.

Fatal Attraction's legacy took a couple of years to become established. The psychosexual thriller really took off in the 1990s with *Basic Instinct* (another Michael Douglas effort), *Sleeping with the Enemy*, *Indecent Proposal* (another Adrian Lyne movie), and *Single White Female*. But for years afterward, men would stop Close in the street and tell her that she saved their marriage. *Sleepless in Seattle* was right: the movie really did scare every man in America.

THE PRINCESS BRIDE

1987

"SHE GETS KIDNAPPED, HE GETS KILLED, BUT IT ALL TURNS OUT OKAY," SAYS *PRINCESS BRIDE* SCREENWRITER WILLIAM GOLDMAN OF HIS BEST-LOVED MOVIE (JUST ABOVE *BUTCH CASSIDY AND THE SUNDANCE KID*).

This is a story about stories, about their power and their strangeness. It's also a story about true love: romantic love, familial love, and abiding friendship. It pokes fun at fairy-tale conventions at exactly the same time that it delivers a classic tale of princesses and pirates and giants and monsters. It's wonderful.

It began with Goldman's book, published in 1973. The following two decades saw numerous attempts to adapt it for the screen, all of which collapsed, sometimes days before production was due to start. Goldman had resigned himself to the idea that it was never going to happen when Rob Reiner got in touch. Following his success with *This Is Spinal Tap* and *The Sure Thing*, Reiner was able to put the pieces, finally, into place, arranging a shoot at London's Shepperton Studios and around England and Ireland, and assembling the only possible cast. Perfect-looking newcomers Cary Elwes and Robin Wright played the star-crossed lovers, with bigger names as moral and comedic support.

The movie is narrated as a book being read by a grandfather (Peter Falk) to his sick grandson (Fred Savage), who would rather be playing computer games. The story the grandfather tells is your typical boy-meets-girl, boy-is-killed-by-pirates, girl-agrees-to-marry-prince-instead, girl-is-kidnapped, pirate-fights-kidnappers-to-win-girl tale, and the grandson is—despite himself—swept up. Buttercup (Wright) and Westley (Elwes) are the young lovers, Chris Sarandon is the handsome but untrustworthy prince, and Christopher Guest is his right-hand man.

The film's real genius is in the trio of kidnappers. There's the blustering, cunning Vizzini (Wallace Shawn); the tormented, grieving Inigo Montoya (Mandy Patinkin); and the giant Fezzik (André the Giant). This eccentric, ragtag gang drag Buttercup across a country and battle, in turn, to keep her away from the pursuing Man in Black, aka the Dread Pirate Roberts.

Of course, the Man in Black is the returning Westley, now tutored by his pirate captors in fencing, fighting, and poison lore. He can swashbuckle with the best of them, and cuts quite a dash in his puffy black shirt. To win Buttercup back, he fights the greatest duel of all time against Inigo, wrestles against Fezzik, and engages in a deadly battle of wits with Vizzini, one of the greatest scenes of the

Above: The story-within-a-story structure of *The Princess Bride* is something plenty of movies have tried, but few have done so with the same success.

Opposite: This was the big break for Robin Wright, who would go on to be a major star of film and TV.

decade. But he must defeat Prince Humperdink and death itself to win his happy ending.

Making the film was not always easy. Wright's dress was set on fire on the first day, and Patinkin and Elwes had to train for months with fencing legends Bob Anderson and Peter Diamond to deliver that showstopping duel. They got so fast with their weapons, in fact, that the first on-set run-through was far too short and at the last minute they had to more than double the length of the duel. Meanwhile, André was in constant pain as a result of the medical condition responsible for his size, and he could not lift any weight without a harness. Yet the set was harmonious, because everyone knew that they were making something special and different. Goldman's script is wildly, showily clever, and its characters delight continually in their own cunning and insight, yet they are so often wrong to do so that it becomes just another running gag when someone smarter shows off. The movie is hilarious (Reiner had to leave the set during Billy Crystal's takes, because his laughing was audible on camera) but it's also wildly romantic, and still unlike anything else.

That's because *The Princess Bride* manages something quietly brilliant, something that few movies have successfully imitated, and that's its bedtime story framing device. The metastory uses the grandson as the skeptical audience for this tale and its biggest on-screen critic. He complains directly to the narrator, and so even the most skeptical, reluctant audience members feel themselves in tune with him. Unconsciously but quickly, they start to trust him to speak for them. And then the movie wins over the grandson and, with him, anyone else who wants to play video games instead of watch this weird movie with the chintzy-sounding title. As Fred Savage's little boy becomes gradually swept up in the quest for true love, even the most cynical among us are swept up right beside him. So almost everyone who watches the movie agrees with Billy Crystal's Miracle Max that, in the end, "True love is the greatest thing in the world." Except—as Max also tells us—for a nice MLT, a mutton, lettuce, and tomato sandwich, of course.

ORIGINAL RELEASE DATE: October 9, 1987 (U.S.); March 25, 1988 (UK)
RUN TIME: 95 minutes

DID YOU KNOW?

- Despite the duels, Mandy Patinkin had only one injury during filming—a bruised rib from holding back laughter in the scenes he shares with Miracle Max (Billy Crystal), because Crystal improvised wildly and filthily for the crew's amusement.

FURTHER VIEWING

- *Willow* (1988)
  George Lucas's fantasy gets a bad rap, but Warwick Davis is an utterly charming lead as the farmer entrusted with the fate of a baby who can bring down an evil witch-queen. His sidekick, Val Kilmer's Madmartigan, is the only swashbuckler of the 1980s to match Westley.

FACTS

"HELLO. MY NAME IS INIGO MONTOYA. YOU KILLED MY FATHER. PREPARE TO DIE."

Inigo Montoya (Mandy Patinkin), *THE PRINCESS BRIDE*

ROBOCOP

1987

IT IS TESTAMENT TO THE GENERAL PREPOSTEROUSNESS OF THE 1980S ACTION MOVIE THAT MOST PEOPLE TOOK *ROBOCOP* SERIOUSLY WHEN IT FIRST CAME OUT, NOT REALIZING THAT PAUL VERHOEVEN'S SCI-FI ACTION THRILLER WAS INTENDED AS A DEVASTATING SATIRE.

It took years for some viewers to catch on and see the suggestion behind the tough-on-crime rhetoric that an inhumane cure for crime is worse than the disease.

Like so many other science-fiction concepts, it can trace its roots to Ridley Scott's *Blade Runner*. Screenwriter Edward Neumeier heard that Scott's movie was about a cop hunting robots, and it got him thinking of a robot cop—one who developed a conscience. Studios shot down the idea, but he happened to meet music video director Michael Miner, who had a similar story about an injured cop who receives cybernetic parts to go back into action. The two men combined their ideas and came up with *RoboCop*.

Director Paul Verhoeven wasn't initially enamored with the idea, but a second look showed him the possibilities. This could have been an almost fascist story, like many incarnations of *Batman* or *Judge Dredd*—infallible supercop destroys crime while dispensing with frivolities such as a full trial and habeas corpus—but instead he undermined it thoroughly by taking aim at corporate greed and a state that has collapsed into oligarchy. SInce then, it has become even more appropriate for the times.

The opening news montage refers to the "Star Wars orbiting peace platform"—barely an exaggeration of Ronald Reagan's then–space policy—and television ads promote fun, family board games called "Nuke 'Em," painting an image of a callous, degraded, and belligerent United States. In the police station, where we meet our ostensible heroes, the steady background noise is that of sobbing, brawling, and punching. Nancy Allen's Officer Anne Lewis is introduced beating up a struggling suspect to demonstrate her toughness— and she's one of the good guys! Her new partner, Peter Weller's Alex J. Murphy, seems a little more caring as he talks about his young son, but his decency has little chance in such a corrupt system.

That is because he's been identified as a prime candidate for the "RoboCop" program at Omni Consumer Products (OCP), the massive and malign company that might as well rule the city. OCP, we are told, has stepped into "markets traditionally regarded as nonprofit: hospitals, prisons, space exploration . . . " As private prisons and health-care giants have discovered in our own world, there is money to be made from the misery of others. If anything, modern audiences might miss this satire, because we've become so accustomed to big businesses swallowing up public enterprises.

However, OCP goes further than most modern corporations, and not just in putting a stock ticker above the urinals. It declares war on the police unions and decides to replace officers with a more high-tech crime fighter. OCP's Dick Jones (Ronny Cox) has been working on the completely robotic ED-209, which unfortunately murders junior executive Mr. Kinney in a hail of gunfire and an extravagant spray of claret at its presentation to the board. "I'm sure it's only a glitch. A temporary setback," Jones assures his bosses, but when they are not reassured, the RoboCop program is okayed instead. Accordingly, across town, Murphy is sent into harm's way, leaving him at least temporarily dead. OCP and project head Bob Morton (Miguel Ferrer) have what they're looking for—human material to build their robot around.

From a dead body, OCP conjures new life: RoboCop. Jones calls him an "unholy monster," echoing Mary Shelley's "hellish monster" and the plot of *Frankenstein*. This modern Prometheus also develops his own moral code and rebels against his masters, although it takes him some time to overcome his (literally) ironclad programming. You can read as much or as little into this as you want. It could be merely an assertion of his recovered individuality or a wider rejection of corporate power and influence, but it's a powerful moment when he introduces himself again as "Murphy."

RoboCop does hunt down the bad guys, clean up the town, and protect and serve the people. But while this movie merrily tells a history of violence, gleefully dissolving one henchman in toxic waste and riddling others with bullets, it's meant to be so over the top that it's absurd (Verhoeven had to cut even more outrageous scenes to get an R rating), and we're meant to understand that these punishments are disproportionate to petty crimes. Finally, it is a reminder to always, *always* read the fine print of your employment contract, or you, too, could end up reanimated to serve corporate ends. After all, Verhoeven was right about the hospitals, prisons, and space program.

Opposite: RoboCop (Peter Weller) steps into action. Dead or alive, criminals are coming with him.

Below: RoboCop brings gangster Clarence Boddicker (Kurtwood Smith) to justice – at least temporarily.

ORIGINAL RELEASE DATE: July 17, 1987 (U.S.); February 5, 1988 (UK)
RUN TIME: 99 minutes

DID YOU KNOW?

◆ The RoboCop costume was so uncomfortable and the Texas weather so warm that Weller lost up to three pounds a day due to sweating in the costume. Later models for the sequels had a built-in fan.

FURTHER VIEWING

◆ *Escape from New York* (1981)
Kurt Russell stars in John Carpenter's politically astute, gleefully absurd sci-fi classic as Snake Plissken, a convict sent in to rescue the U.S. president from a terrifying supermax prison: Manhattan.

FACTS

BEST MUSICAL MOMENTS OF THE 1980S

As long as you were okay with synthesizers and not allergic to hairspray, the 1980s was a great decade for music. Pop got a boost from the arrival of MTV, rock splintered into a thousand flamboyant pieces (hair metal, heavy metal, punk), and rap started small but grew to take over the world. Yet some of the best musical moments on film were throwbacks to the 1950s or 1960s. It just goes to show that nostalgia isn't what it used to be.

SAY ANYTHING . . . (1989)
THE SONG: "IN YOUR EYES," PETER GABRIEL

John Cusack plays an underachiever dating the high school valedictorian; after she dumps him, he tries to woo her back with the power of Peter Gabriel, standing under her window to deliver a boom-box serenade. Romeo, eat your heart out.

PRETTY IN PINK (1986)
THE SONG: "TRY A LITTLE TENDERNESS," OTIS REDDING

Perhaps the best lip-synching ever committed to film, Ducky (Jon Cryer) gives his all in a casual, mad, joyous performance of Otis Redding's slow-building banger. Of course, Molly Ringwald's Andie just stares at him, because she is awful.

FERRIS BUELLER'S DAY OFF (1986)
THE SONG: "TWIST AND SHOUT," THE BEATLES

Having seen all the most famous sights, eaten at the best restaurants, and kissed the prettiest girl, how else could Matthew Broderick's Ferris Bueller finish his day but by leading a parade down Michigan Avenue, dancing to this catchiest of Beatles recordings?

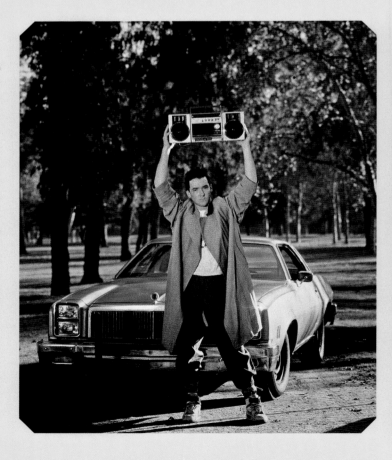

PEE-WEE'S BIG ADVENTURE (1985)
THE SONG: "TEQUILA," THE CHAMPS

Having wandered into the wrong biker gang bar and accidentally knocked over all their bikes, Pee-Wee Herman (Paul Reubens) is facing certain death. He wins a reprieve, somehow, by dancing to "Tequila" along the top of a bar and smashing the gang's drinks. Don't try this at home, kids.

RISKY BUSINESS (1983)
THE SONG: "OLD TIME ROCK 'N' ROLL," BOB SEGER

When the parents are away, the teens will play. Tom Cruise's Joel celebrates his first night of freedom with a whiskey and coke, a TV dinner, and a no-holds-barred dance around the living room in shirt, underpants, and white sports socks. Somehow, it made him a star.

DO THE RIGHT THING (1989)
THE SONG: "FIGHT THE POWER," PUBLIC ENEMY

On a hot summer's day, racial tensions boil over in a pizzeria as Public Enemy blasts out. The moment after Sal (Danny Aiello) attacks Radio Raheem's (Bill Nunn) boom box and absolute silence descends is somehow more shocking than all the swearing before it.

BLUE VELVET (1986)
THE SONG: "IN DREAMS," ROY ORBISON

This is another case of lip-synching, but a far more disturbing one. Ben (Dean Stockwell) performs Ray Orbison's melancholy classic, first entrancing and then enraging his violent partner in crime, Frank (Dennis Hopper). It's surreal, unsettling, and strangely beautiful.

DIRTY DANCING (1987)
THE SONG: "(I'VE HAD) THE TIME OF MY LIFE," BILL MEDLEY AND JENNIFER WARNES

An Oscar, Grammy, and Golden Globe winner, the song was the soundtrack for the joyous, brilliantly choreographed dance finale when Baby came out of the corner and onto the stage. There's rarely a moment where it has not been played, somewhere in the world, ever since.

BACK TO THE FUTURE (1985)
THE SONG: "JOHNNY B. GOODE," CHUCK BERRY

Michael J. Fox's Marty McFly steps in to perform with Marvin Berry and the Starlighters, so his parents-to-be can have their first dance, and rocks out with a classic rock 'n' roll hit. Marvin, meanwhile, gets on the phone to his cousin Chuck to tell him he's found this new sound.

ROCKY III (1983)
THE SONG: "EYE OF THE TIGER," SURVIVOR

Sylvester Stallone wanted Queen's "Another One Bites the Dust" and actually turned down Joe Esposito's "You're the Best," which went to *The Karate Kid* instead. But it turned out for the best. "Eye of the Tiger" became the best *Rocky* theme and something of a theme song for the decade.

Opposite: John Cusack's Lloyd Dobler attempts to win back lone Skye's Diane with the power of Peter Gabriel's "In Your Eyes." The film comes from director Cameron Crowe, who would go on to make similarly music-themed hits like *Almost Famous*.

Above: Michael J. Fox rocks out on stage and changes the course of history in the process.

DIRTY DANCING

1987

A LOT OF MOVIES AIMED AT WOMEN ARE DISMISSED AS FLUFF OR TRASH, AND *DIRTY DANCING* IS NO EXCEPTION.

The movie was a huge success. It was the first film to sell more than a million copies on home VHS, and the soundtrack albums went multiplatinum, spending eighteen weeks at the top of the *Billboard* chart. The standout single "(I've Had) the Time of My Life," by Bill Medley and Jennifer Warnes, won an Oscar, a Golden Globe, and a Grammy. Despite the enormous success it had, it's still dismissed as a chick flick—but strip away the pretty prom dresses and stage makeup, and this is a tough story about love across the class divide, the emotional violence of economic insecurity, and the price you pay to grow up.

The main story arc is a coming of age for Jennifer Grey's Frances "Baby" Houseman, the daddy's girl who has always reveled in her parents' approval, as she spends the summer after high school at a resort in the Catskills mountains in New York with her family. To the extent that Baby ever rebels, it's only in dressing in shapeless cardigans and caring about politics in a way that sets her apart from her flightier, more flirtatious sister. Personally, she's a pushover, even going on dates uncomplaining with the condescending Neil (Lonny Price).

But something changes when Baby sees Johnny Castle (Patrick Swayze), wearing one of motion-

Above: Baby (Jennifer Grey) and Johnny (Patrick Swayze) practice their lifts in a lake, all the better to cushion awkward landings.

Opposite: The film's final dance number made "(I've Had) the Time of My Life" a worldwide hit, and sparked endless copycat performances on TV dance shows and for ambitious newlyweds.

picture history's better mullets and dancing with his professional partner Penny Johnson (Cynthia Rhodes). Her reaction is not just a sexual awakening (although that's part of it) but a personal one. She's fascinated by this beautiful and uninhibited pair, fascinated by the wild dancing among the staff kids after the guests go to bed. Baby's high ideals and sheltered existence come crashing down against reality when she learns of Penny's unplanned pregnancy. She asks her beloved dad (Jerry Orbach) for the money for a backstreet abortion, but unless someone can dance in Penny's place at a gala event, both dancers will be out of work. Johnny tells Baby she can't step in and help, and steel appears in her eyes for the first time. Soon she's stripped down to tights and a tube top, sweating her heart out in a rehearsal studio, and saving the day.

As she learns to dance, they fall in love—as is inevitable, because movies about dancing make clear that it's the vertical expression of a horizontal desire. And that romance is powered by an all-time great soundtrack, full of 1960s classics and 1980s pop and even a Patrick Swayze ballad—a better mix than it perhaps sounds. But the movie never loses sight of the wider world, even in a haze of romance. Max Cantor's obnoxious, Ayn Rand–reading waiter Robbie (the man responsible for Penny's crisis) neatly sums up the divide when he callously claims that "some people count; some people don't." In a he-said/she-said situation, Robbie knows his denial will always be believed over Penny's claims.

Our heroes, Johnny and Baby, are also divided by class, and money. She's a valued guest at the resort; he's the hired help, threatened with being fired for even minor infractions. At the end of the summer, she'll go to the prestigious Mount Holyoke College, while he will return to New York as part of the House Painters and Plasterers Union. Class shadows every aspect of their relationship, yet they fall in love anyway. Incidentally, it's worth noting that Baby is the one who makes the first move, in a seduction scene that is designed to appeal to female viewers instead of the traditional male gaze. But female empowerment or not, the course of true love doesn't run smooth, and when their affair comes out, it's Johnny who catches the heat. If he leaves quietly, he'll still get his summer bonus.

It's that dark context that makes the love story shine so brightly, and that ordeal that gives the final happy ending its wings. Johnny doesn't go quietly, but comes back to interrupt the world's worst talent show, reclaim Baby, earn her father's respect, and stand up to the Man, via the medium of dance. The final dance routine owes little to the 1960s setting, and far more to the 1980s of the movie, but it's glorious. Literally and figuratively uplifting, it's a revolt against the system that separates them, an assertion of equality, and an extremely rhythmic representation of hope for a better world. The wild romance that comes with the statement "nobody puts Baby in a corner" is just a bonus.

ORIGINAL RELEASE DATE: August 21, 1987 (U.S.); October 16, 1987 (UK)
RUN TIME: 100 minutes

DID YOU KNOW?

♦ Screenwriter and producer Eleanor Bergstein based the story on her own teenage years, dirty dancing in friends' basements. The script was repeatedly rejected until Vestron Pictures picked it up.

FURTHER VIEWING

♦ *Footloose* (1984)
Another tale of standing up to the Man via the medium of dance, but here Kevin Bacon's rebellious teen convinces a small town government to overturn a total ban of dance, and he also plays chicken with tractors.

FACTS

THE LOST BOYS

1987

SLEEP ALL DAY. PARTY ALL NIGHT. YOU'LL NEVER GROW OLD, AND YOU'LL NEVER DIE.

But you must feed. Vampirism is an appealing prospect, right up to the bloodsucking part, and *The Lost Boys* makes it look like even more of a blast than most movies about the sexiest breed of undead.

The film opens with teenager Michael (Jason Patric), his younger brother Sam (Corey Haim), and their mom Lucy (Dianne Wiest) moving to the small California town of Santa Carla (Santa Cruz by another name). Sam sports frosted tips and giant, fluorescent shirts, while the older and moodier Michael is going for more of a James Dean vibe. But when they go looking for new friends, Michael unwisely fixes on the gorgeous Starr (Jami Gertz), who runs with a bad crowd. Like, bloodsucking bad. Under the charismatic David (Kiefer Sutherland), these guys may have cool bikes and weird powers, but that's only because they're feeding on the unwary. Soon, David has drawn Michael into his orbit and power, and he stands in danger of being turned into a vampire. Luckily for everyone, Sam has befriended the eccentric Frog brothers, Edgar (Corey Feldman) and Alan (Jamison Newlander), who have a plan to fight back.

Plot-wise, then, it's basically a lifetime movie about the dangers of joining a gang of teenage delinquents; there is little to distinguish the Lost Boys and, say, *The Karate Kid*'s Cobra Kai. Both groups wear cool leather jackets, ride dirt bikes, and disrupt other people's beach parties. The only real distinction is that the Cobra Kai stop short of literal bloodsucking. Even the more supernatural elements here—the "maggot" rice and noodles that appear like worms— play out like fraternity hazing rituals instead of the monster initiation rites they prove to be. However, while this movie dips into horror, it doesn't stint on

the blood, giving the audience the jolt of gore they need to convince teen viewers that this is mature and a little dangerous.

That's all thanks to director Joel Schumacher. The movie was originally conceived as a *Goonies*-like adventure for Richard Donner to direct, with a thirteen-to-fourteen-year-old gang of vampires and two eight-year-old Boy Scouts as the Frog brothers. The original script was modeled on *Peter Pan* and even called the Emerson family Michael, John, and Wendy, with David as Peter, the lost boy looking for a mother for his gang. When Donner moved on to make *Lethal Weapon* (although he still produced), Schumacher stepped in on condition that the movie be aged up to allow for a little more sex and violence. He brought in Jeffrey Boam, the screenwriter who worked on the *Lethal Weapon* sequels and *Indiana*

Above: Corey Haim's Sam quickly befriends the Frog brothers, Alan (Jamison Newlander) and Edgar (Corey Feldman).

Opposite: The film's stylish black, white, and red poster, which squeezes in Jason Patric's Michael and Corey Haim's Sam.

Jones and the Last Crusade, to rewrite the story, and ended up with a teen vampire movie as funny as these vampires' mullets.

It's also packed with memorable characters. The boys' eccentric, Willie Nelson–like grandpa (Barnard Hughes) gets the film's final laugh, but Wiest's shy, kind Lucy is charming (this was her follow-up to her Oscar win for *Hannah and Her Sisters*), and her relationship with Edward Herrmann's nerdy, apparently kindly Max is sweet. Sam and the Frog brothers may occasionally shout too much—especially when fleeing vampires—but their comic geekery and perpetual panic makes them entertaining all the same, and their banter mixes high and low stakes beautifully. The movie also has about 90 percent of a really cool soundtrack, and 10 percent a topless guy in purple leggings playing the sax, perhaps the most 1980s image ever committed to celluloid.

At the other end of the charm scale are the vampires, led by Kiefer Sutherland's bleach-haired, spiky David. Go back to the movie and you'll realize that David isn't on-screen much, perhaps 10 minutes of the total running time. But with his unblinking stare and that dangerous attitude, his presence looms far larger. And things get seriously gory. Sam's husky Nanook knocks one vampire (Alexander Bacan Chapman) into a bath of holy water, with grotesque consequences for plumbing all over the house. Sam shoots another (Billy Wirth) and impales him on a hi-fi ("Death by stereo!") that somehow explodes. The effects are limited and often shoddy, relying heavily on swooping cameras and invisible threats. But the vampire prosthetics are elegant, courtesy of future Oscar winner Greg Cannom (who would return to vampires in 1999 for *Blade*). Even these exaggerated cheekbones and foreheads reinforce the idea that vampirehood might be fun. You get to stay young, jump off bridges, fly, and hang out with Edward Herrmann. Maybe sucking blood would be worth it.

ORIGINAL RELEASE DATE: July 31, 1987 (U.S.)
RUN TIME: 97 minutes

DID YOU KNOW?

- Tim Cappello, the buff saxophonist who plays "I Still Believe," also appears in the video for Tina Turner's "We Don't Need Another Hero," the theme for *Mad Max: Beyond Thunderdome*.

FURTHER VIEWING

- *Near Dark* (1987)
  In the same year, Kathryn Bigelow's vampire Western told a similar story of semi-transformed vampires fighting for their humanity, only with less humor and a lot more cool. Funnily enough, the kid vampire there is played by Jason Patric's younger brother, Joshua Miller.

FACTS

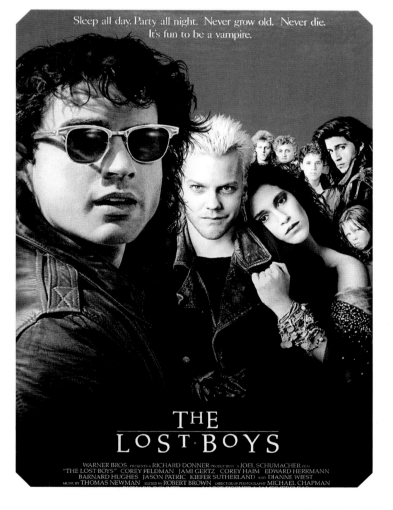

Sleep all day. Party all night. Never grow old. Never die. It's fun to be a vampire.

THE LOST BOYS

WARNER BROS. PRESENTS A RICHARD DONNER PRODUCTION A JOEL SCHUMACHER FILM
"THE LOST BOYS" COREY FELDMAN JAMI GERTZ COREY HAIM EDWARD HERRMANN
BARNARD HUGHES JASON PATRIC KIEFER SUTHERLAND AND DIANNE WIEST
MUSIC BY THOMAS NEWMAN EDITED BY ROBERT BROWN DIRECTOR OF PHOTOGRAPHY MICHAEL CHAPMAN

1988 HIGHLIGHTS

It was all about high concept: big ideas, great execution. What if Hollywood's biggest and smallest stars were twins? What if Bruce Willis jumped off a skyscraper? What if cartoons lived among us? Meanwhile, Tom Cruise proved he could combine box-office dominance with serious acting talent and Tom Hanks began his climb to Oscar glory.

HIGHEST-GROSSING FILMS (U.S.)

1. *Rain Man*	United Artists	$172,825,435
2. *Who Framed Roger Rabbit*	Disney	$156,452,370
3. *Coming to America*	Paramount	$128,152,301
4. *Big*	20th Century Fox	$114,968,774
5. *Twins*	Universal	$111,938,388
6. *Crocodile Dundee II*	Paramount	$109,306,210
7. *Die Hard*	20th Century Fox	$83,008,852
8. *The Naked Gun: From the Files of Police Squad!*	Paramount	$78,756,177
9. *Cocktail*	Disney	$78,222,753
10. *Beetlejuice*	Warner Bros.	$73,707,461

AT THE GOLDEN GLOBES

Best Picture (Drama)	*Rain Man*
Best Picture (Comedy/Musical)	*Working Girl*
Best Director	Clint Eastwood, *Bird*
Best Actor (Drama)	Dustin Hoffman, *Rain Man*
Best Actor (Comedy/Musical)	Tom Hanks, *Big*
Best Actress (Drama)	Jodie Foster, *The Accused*;
	Sigourney Weaver, *Gorillas in the Mist*;
	Shirley MacLaine, *Madame Sousatzka* (tie)
Best Actress (Comedy/Musical)	Melanie Griffith, *Working Girl*

CANNES FILM FESTIVAL

Palme d'Or winner
Pelle the Conqueror,
Bille August

NOTABLE DEATHS

Trevor Howard, January 7	Actor, *The Third Man* and *Brief Encounter*
Emeric Pressburger, February 5	Screenwriter and director, *A Matter of Life and Death* and *The Red Shoes*
Kenneth Williams, April 15	Actor, *Carry On Up the Khyber* and *Carry On Cleo*
John Carradine, November 27	Actor, *Stagecoach* and *The Ten Commandments*
Hal Ashby, December 27	Airector, *Harold and Maude* and *Being There*

AT THE OSCARS

Best Picture	*Rain Man*
Best Director	Barry Levinson, *Rain Man*
Best Actor	Dustin Hoffman, *Rain Man*
Best Actress	Jodie Foster, *The Accused*

THIS YEAR'S BIG OSCARS INJUSTICE

In retrospect, Tom Cruise's performance in *Rain Man* looks maybe even better than Hoffman's, and he didn't even get a nomination.

FUTURE MOVIE STAR BIRTHS

June 7: Michael Cera, *Scott Pilgrim vs. The World* and *Juno*
August 24: Rupert Grint, *Harry Potter* series and *Cherrybomb*
October 3: Alicia Vikander, *The Danish Girl* and *Tomb Raider*
November 6: Emma Stone, *La La Land* and *Battle of the Sexes*
December 1: Zoe Kravitz, *X-Men: First Class* and *Mad Max: Fury Road*

NOTABLE FILM DEBUTS

Annette Bening, *The Great Outdoors*
Matt Damon, *Mystic Pizza*
Alan Rickman, *Die Hard*
Julia Roberts, *Satisfaction*
Uma Thurman, *Johnny Be Good*
Benicio Del Toro, *Big Top Pee-Wee*

DIE HARD

THROUGHOUT THE LATE 1980S AND EARLY 1990S, THERE WAS A STRING OF ACTION MOVIES IN WHICH TERRORISTS TOOK CONTROL OF A PLACE OR THING.

There was *Die Hard* on a boat (*Under Siege*), *Die Hard* on a plane (*Passenger 57*), *Die Hard* on the president's plane (*Air Force One*). Terrorists attacked a train (*Under Siege 2*), an airport (*Die Hard 2*), and the city of New York (*Die Hard with a Vengeance*). All of them were trying to mimic or improve one unmatchable film—the perfect action movie. But there's only one *Die Hard*, and even its own sequels never measured up.

The story is—like its hero—straightforward and muscular. NYPD cop John McClane (Bruce Willis)

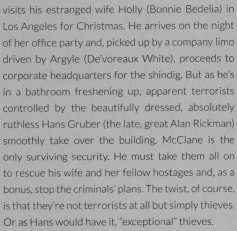

visits his estranged wife Holly (Bonnie Bedelia) in Los Angeles for Christmas. He arrives on the night of her office party and, picked up by a company limo driven by Argyle (De'voreaux White), proceeds to corporate headquarters for the shindig. But as he's in a bathroom freshening up, apparent terrorists controlled by the beautifully dressed, absolutely ruthless Hans Gruber (the late, great Alan Rickman) smoothly take over the building. McClane is the only surviving security. He must take them all on to rescue his wife and her fellow hostages and, as a bonus, stop the criminals' plans. The twist, of course, is that they're not terrorists at all but simply thieves. Or as Hans would have it, "exceptional" thieves.

The one-man-stands-alone element had been done, of course, in everything from *Shane* to *Rambo*, and the single-location action movie was almost equally familiar. But something about the combination in *Die Hard* proved remarkably effective, the claustrophobic setup amping up the stakes. McClane couldn't escape even if he wanted to, nor can anyone else get in to reinforce him without endangering the hostages. And his separation from outside law enforcement makes for communication issues and disbelief on their part, leaving him not only fighting the hostage-takers but also the authorities outside. Because the terrorists have anticipated every response to their plan, he's the only wild card who can change the outcome.

More important, McClane's a great action hero because, while his instincts are flawless, the movie puts him through the wringer. He's barefoot, so the terrorists shoot the glass and leave him walking on torn feet. It's not enough that he has to escape

Left: Nobody has managed to make a white tank top look as rugged and manly since Bruce Willis stripped down to his while defending the Nakatomi Plaza.

Opposite: Bloodstained and barefoot—McClane was an action movie tough guy who took more than his fair share of punishment.

a soon-to-blow rooftop by rappelling off on a fire hose; he then has to scramble his way out of the hose when its reel threatens to pull him back off the building. Not only does he shoot Hans, but he also has to stop him from pulling Holly out the window with him by the strap of her new Rolex. His trials only build, relentlessly, until the credits roll.

Bruce Willis wasn't the original choice for the film—Sylvester Stallone, Harrison Ford, and Don Johnson all turned it down—but director John McTiernan went to bat for him, based on the success of his TV show *Moonlighting* and his last movie, *Blind Date*, and it is now impossible to imagine anyone else as this put-upon hero. He is an incomparable man's man in his filthy undershirt and with his gun belt, and his gleam is only burnished by comparison to weasely yuppie Harry Ellis (Hart Bochner) and the mostly long-haired Eurotrash criminals. McClane's only outside ally, sergeant Al Powell (Reginald VelJohnson), has a personal arc that plays off the New York cop's machismo, too. Al is desk-bound after wrongly shooting a teenager; the movie's final action beat sees him get his mojo back by executing a terrorist. It's an odd kind of redemption.

And then there is Hans Gruber. This was Alan Rickman's first movie after making an impressive start to his career on stage, and there have been few debuts as emphatic. From the moment he strolls out of the elevator, flanked by goons and wearing a small smile above his custom-tailored suit, he seems in complete control of the situation and his men, who run from the unhinged (Alexander Godunov's Karl) to gleefully sociopathic (Clarence Gllyard's Theo).

McClane takes out the gang anyway, of course, because one man with a revolver and bare feet always trumps a gang with machine guns and rocket launchers in action-movie logic. Even with bare and bleeding feet, even exhausted and bruised and covered in filth, the righteous man can always triumph over the greedy. Perhaps that is especially true at Christmas, when this film is set. It is, as Hans Gruber reminds us, a time for miracles.

ORIGINAL RELEASE DATE: July 20, 1988 (U.S.); February 3, 1989 (UK)
RUN TIME: 127 minutes

DID YOU KNOW?
- The building that plays Nakatomi Plaza is in fact Fox Plaza, then under construction as the new headquarters of the studio 20th Century Fox. Studio bosses okayed its use, but got a little nervous when they saw just how many explosives were involved. Fortunately, it's still standing thirty years later.

FURTHER VIEWING
- *Witness* (1985)
  An obscure link this time, but Alexander Godunov also appears as a likable farmer in this gripping thriller set among the Amish, in which Harrison Ford tries to protect Kelly McGillis and Lukas Haas after they witness a murder.

FACTS

BEETLEJUICE

1988

THIS WASN'T TIM BURTON'S FIRST MOVIE, BUT IT'S THE FIRST ONE THAT FEELS LIKE A TIM BURTON MOVIE. AFTER THE GENERALLY CHEERFUL *PEE-WEE'S BIG ADVENTURE* BECAME A HIT, BURTON SUDDENLY HAD THE FREEDOM TO MAKE A MORE PERSONAL FILM.

So naturally he made a story about ghosts, monster ghosts, a little Goth girl, and her awful, awful family. Start as you mean to go on, after all. The story begins with Adam (Alec Baldwin) and his wife Barbara Maitland (Geena Davis). This sweet, unassuming couple lives in a beautiful old house in the small New England town of Winter River, Connecticut. They're preparing a stay-cation to spend more time on her decorating and his train sets—until, shockingly, they drive off a bridge and die. It's an abrupt shift of tone from cutesy to creepy, and suddenly the viewer realizes that we're in a different movie than we thought. We're in Tim Burton's world now.

As the couple are struggling to adjust to the afterlife and wading through the "Handbook for the Newly Deceased," their home is sold to a family from New York. Charles Deetz (Jeffrey Jones) plans for a quiet life in the country, at least until he buys up the entire town for his boss. Delia (Catherine O'Hara) wants to redecorate and turn the place into an art center, and their daughter Lydia (Winona Ryder) is a weird little Goth who just wants to take photos in peace, preferably far away from either of her parents. It's Lydia who makes first contact with the Maitlands, and she's far too cool to be scared by ghosts. She is, after all, Winona Ryder. "I myself am strange and unusual," claims Lydia, and certainly she's a lot more alarming-looking than either of the resident ghosts, with her short, spiky bangs and entirely black wardrobe.

The Maitlands try to scare the Deetzes away, but their efforts fall short. Their somewhat sweet, all-out attempt—possessing Delia and her dinner-party guests and forcing them to dance to Harry Belafonte's "Day-O"—goes wrong because it's so much better than the hosts' usual dinner parties.

So, in desperation, they call on "bio-exterminator" Beetlejuice (Michael Keaton). This turns out to be a mistake. Beetlejuice has none of the Maitlands' restraint and positively delights in terrifying the humans. Even Lydia is freaked out when he appears, needle-toothed, on a giant rattlesnake's body. Beetlejuice is a huckster, a weirdo, and a psycho, with crazy hair and patches of green mold growing all over his pasty face. He can shapeshift at will and play malevolent tricks on the living and the dead, and he enjoys that almost as much as he enjoys visiting undead brothels (Dante's Inferno Rooms) or kicking back with a cold drink of a kind that we shouldn't inquire about too closely.

So many of Burton's preoccupations are already present that this seems like a distillation of all his later work. There are the monstrous machines that transform the house, and a Danny Elfman score that's heavy on French horn and tuba. There are Michael Keaton, and Winona Ryder, and a sufficiently large selection of carousels and insects and eyeballs to creep anyone out. The afterlife, in this incarnation, is full of blue- and green-shaded pinup girls with pink hair, dark shadowed eyes, and scars on their wrists. In the waiting room of the dead, a bisected girl sits next to a man with a shrunken head and a charred corpse. Many of these ideas recur to some degree in Burton's other movies and his books, such as *The Melancholy Death of Oyster Boy*, while Adam and Barbara's monster selves look like something out of *The Nightmare Before Christmas* or possibly one of the fantastically detailed but disturbing paintings by the fifteenth-century Dutch painter Hieronymus Bosch.

Beetlejuice tries to persuade Lydia to marry him in exchange for his help with the Maitlands, but they rescue her from his clutches before she's united with the moldy ghost for good. And the Deetzes, chastened by their contact with the undead, allow the Maitlands to restore the house and essentially adopt Lydia. It's a surprisingly happy ending, given all the movie's disturbing jokes about suicide and portrayal of an afterlife full of people cursed to remain in very much the situation in which they were killed. Then again, that's been Burton's approach ever since. He gives us the weird and wonderful, but he undercuts it with the sense that the dead are just as likable, and insecure, as we are. Delia complains at one point here that "they're dead; it's a little late to be neurotic," but Burton's whole career has been built on the idea that that's not true. The dead, the monsters, and the freaks are just as screwed up as the rest of us, and that's okay by him.

Opposite: Despite his understandable top billing, Keaton has relatively little screen time. What he has, though, he makes the most of.

Below: Keaton's Beetlejuice at the altar with Winona Ryder, who became the film's breakout star.

ORIGINAL RELEASE DATE: March 30, 1988 (U.S.); August 19, 1988 (UK)
RUN TIME: 92 minutes

DID YOU KNOW?

- The original script was more of a horror movie and Beetlejuice was a demon who disguised himself as an old man, explicitly intending to kill the Deetzes instead of merely frightening them away.

FURTHER VIEWING

- *Dune* (1984)
  If you felt that *Beetlejuice* was too comic and really needed more sand dunes and giant worms, try David Lynch's different (but almost equally weird) adaptation of Frank Herbert's sci-fi classic.

FACTS

A FISH CALLED WANDA

1988

THE ACADEMY AWARDS GENERALLY OVERLOOK COMEDIES.

No matter how good your performance or how inspired your script, it will usually be ignored unless you hang the laughs on some serious social issues. However, *A Fish Called Wanda* was an exception. Despite being a delightful crime farce, it was nominated for three Oscars and Kevin Kline won Best Supporting Actor for his inspired portrayal of the worst man in the world.

Plot-wise, it's a heist-gone-right movie. Con woman Wanda (Jamie Lee Curtis) and her deranged boyfriend Otto (Kevin Kline) have teamed up with animal lover Ken (Michael Palin) and gangster George Thomason (Tom Georgeson) to steal a fortune in diamonds. But when George hides the diamonds just before he's sent to prison, Wanda must scramble to find the hiding place and double-cross at least two of the three men so she can keep the loot for herself.

Somehow, respectable barrister Archie Leach (John Cleese) finds himself caught up in it all. He is George's trial lawyer, so Wanda hopes that George will tell him where the diamonds are hidden, and that she can seduce him into sharing the information. But the reserved, somewhat uptight Archie refuses to even talk to her, given that she's George's alibi, so she has her work cut out—for about a minute and a half, until her obvious attractiveness wins out.

There is a lot of fun, culture-clash humor, with Archie explaining the strict rules of the English legal system to a horrified Wanda, and with Otto meeting Archie's offer to box like a gentleman by picking up a gun like a good American. As you might expect from a leading light of *Monty Python's Flying Circus*, Cleese's script is full of zingers, with lines such as

Left: Jamie Lee Curtis shook off her "scream queen" title to build a successful career in comedy.

"He's so dumb that he thought that the Gettysburg Address was where Lincoln lived."

Most important, the performances are dead-on. Curtis is adorable and absolutely ruthless in the lead, wrapping every man she meets around her little finger and double-crossing them as soon as possible. Cleese is pleasantly bewildered, as is Palin (although with a spectacular stutter). Palin's story line, about an animal lover whose attempts to murder a witness keep resulting in the deaths of small, adorable creatures, is hilarious. But Kline stands out as Otto, a living embodiment of the Dunning-Kruger effect. He's heavily armed and entirely impulsive, which is rarely a good combination.

The movie was directed by Charles Crichton, although Cleese had to name himself as "codirector" to get the film insurance, because the studio was worried by the seventy-eight-year-old Crichton's age. The veteran moviemaker was responsible for one of the finest comedies of the 1940s, Ealing Studio's *The Lavender Hill Mob*, which starred Alec Guinness as a mild-mannered bank clerk who made off with a fortune in gold bars. However, he hadn't directed a movie in twenty-three years, working in television and in training films, through which he met Cleese, who was the actor that lured him back to the crime-comedy crossover genre. They worked together on the film's story from 1983, each contributing favorite ideas to the mix. Cleese liked the idea of a stutterer who desperately wanted to tell his captors information but couldn't get the words out; Crichton offered that someone should be run over by a steamroller.

And, unlike in *The Lavender Hill Mob*, where the villain was nabbed in an ending mandated by the Moral Majority, crime does pay in *A Fish Called Wanda*. According to the end titles, all the major characters live happily ever after. Archie and Wanda "were married in Rio, had seventeen children, and founded a leper colony," while Ken got to work with the fishes and "Otto emigrated to [apartheid] South Africa and became Minister of Justice," the only job that's close to being as awful as he is. It was such a perfect sign-off, in fact, that the team could never settle on a follow-up, so they made a

ORIGINAL RELEASE DATE: July 15, 1988 (U.S.); October 14, 1988 (UK)
RUN TIME: 104 minutes

DID YOU KNOW?

- John Cleese's character's name, Archie Leach, is the real name of Hollywood legend Cary Grant. Cleese claimed it was the closest he could ever get to being Cary Grant.

FURTHER VIEWING

- *Trading Places* (1983)
  Jamie Lee Curtis starred in one other iconic comedy in the 1980s, John Landis's *Trading Places*, in which she's a hooker with a heart of gold who helps Dan Aykroyd's former rich kid team up with Eddie Murphy's former hustler to get revenge on those who wronged them.

FACTS

"spiritual sequel" with different characters in 1997's relatively disappointing *Fierce Creatures*.

But a comedy this well constructed is always hard to replicate. For the torture scene alone, where Otto tries to wring information from Ken by eating his pet fish one by one ("Avoid the green ones. They're not ripe yet."), this belongs among the funniest movies ever put on-screen, and it teaches us several important lessons. It's useful to learn a foreign language, because it may help your sex life, and you should never eat another man's fish.

Below: The cast line up for questioning in this promotional poster for the movie.

BEST FOREIGN MOVIES OF THE 1980S

Not all great movies—some critics would claim not even many great movies—hail from Hollywood. The 1980s saw the rise of the hyperstylized *Cinema du Look* in France, which influenced the United States for decades after, and the explosion of Spanish cinema led by the colorful, daring Pedro Almodóvar. In Japan, the animation industry pushed the boundaries of what was possible for the art form and inspired generations of artists. Here are a few of the best international movies:

RAN (1985)

The legendary Akira Kurosawa considered this his finest movie, combining elements of Shakespeare's *King Lear* with the Japanese tale of Mōri Motonari to tell the epic story of a warlord's struggle with his three warrior sons.

SUBWAY (1985)

Luc Besson's first contribution to *Cinema du Look*, the movie stars Christophe Lambert as a peroxide-blond thief/tramp/pop star having an affair with a gangster's girlfriend. It's not sensible, but it's superbly cool.

MY NEIGHBOR TOTORO (1988)

Arguably Hayao Miyazaki's finest movie (and setting a high bar for all that followed), this gentle fantasy sees two small girls befriending a strange forest spirit. There's emotion under the whimsy—their mother is being treated for a serious illness—but it's still gloriously uplifting.

Left: The Catbus, Totoro, and Satsuki from Hayao Miyazaki's glorious *My Neighbor Totoro*. No other bus will ever live up to this mode of transportation.

Opposite: Jinpachi Nezu as Jiro in Akira Kurosawa's *Ran*. The director used color to easily distinguish the three competing warlords fighting for their father's crown.

WINGS OF DESIRE (1987)

An angel falls in love with a circus performer and reconsiders his immortality in Wim Wenders's dreamy fairy tale. In one of the greatest casting decisions ever, he takes advice from a former angel: Peter Falk (played by the actor Peter Falk as himself). Of course Columbo is an angel.

WOMEN ON THE VERGE OF A NERVOUS BREAKDOWN (1988)

This riotous comedy about adultery, attempted suicide, terrorism, and mental illness brought director Pedro Almodóvar to international attention. Carmen Maura is a woman who's been dumped by her lover—but it turns out that's the least of her problems.

CINEMA PARADISO (1988)

Giuseppe Tornatore's Oscar winner talks about nostalgia and the magic of cinema, ending with a montage of kisses censored from decades of movies that will reduce any film fan to tears.

THE KILLER (1989)

An influence on Quentin Tarantino, among others, John Woo's gritty crime thriller sees Chow Yun Fat as a repentant assassin. Drawing from the French New Wave, it instead became a new high for Hong Kong cinema.

FITZCARRALDO (1982)

The story of a nineteenth-century dreamer who moved a steamship over a mountain in the Amazon, this movie was an act of similar wild ambition that nearly drove director Werner Herzog and his famously difficult leading man Klaus Kinski mad.

JEAN DE FLORETTE (1986)

Three of France's biggest stars—Yves Montand, Gerard Depardieu, and Daniel Auteuil—give life to this strangely gripping account of neighborly squabbles over a stream. Watch it with the sequel, *Manon des Sources*.

AKIRA (1988)

The disappearance of a boy in futuristic Neo-Tokyo leads his friends to discover a mind-boggling conspiracy in one of the most influential sci-fi movies or animated films of all time. Katsuhiro Otomo's masterpiece is cosmic in scope.

Left: Damiel (Bruno Ganz) and Marion (Solveig Dommartin) in Wim Wenders's *Wings of Desire*.

Below: Gerard Depardieu as the titular hunchbacked character Jean de Florette.

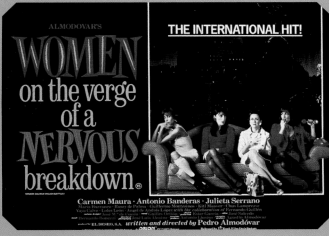

Top: Alfredo (Philippe Noiret) and six-year-old "Totò" (Salvatore Cascio) in the projection room of *Cinema Paradiso*.

Bottom left: The poster for Pedro Almodovar's breakthrough comic hit, *Women on the Verge of a Nervous Breakdown*.

Bottom right: Chow Yun Fat in John Woo's *The Killer*.

WHO FRAMED ROGER RABBIT

1988

A PRACTICALLY PERFECT FILM ABOUT THE MAGIC OF MOVIES, *WHO FRAMED ROGER RABBIT* WAS THE FIRST HERALD OF THE DISNEY ANIMATION RENAISSANCE THAT WOULD PEAK DURING THE 1990S.

But this Robert Zemeckis movie is also its own, unique triumph, a never-bettered mix of live-action and traditional animation in a story that also blends noir tropes and *Looney Tunes* mayhem. The title's missing question mark is about its only flaw.

The concept is simple genius. Toons are real, and they interact with the real world. So Daffy and Donald Duck can play a nightclub piano duet (that ends up more of a piano duel); Dumbo can be loaned out to a rival studio; and a cartoon bunny called Roger Rabbit (voiced by Charles Fleischer) can be framed for the murder of Marvin Acme (Stubby Kaye), head of the Acme Corporation that once supplied Wile E. Coyote. Uniting these characters was a major legal challenge for the moviemakers; Mickey Mouse and Bugs Bunny had to have equal prominence; Daffy and Donald had to be equally skilled pianists; Popeye wasn't featured because even executive producer Steven Spielberg couldn't persuade King Features to allow him in. It's still the only such crossover ever made.

Our human hero is Bob Hoskins's Eddie Valiant, a private eye down on his luck. Eddie hasn't been the same since the unsolved murder of his brother and partner by a wild-eyed 'toon, and he now scrapes a living covering seedy divorces and avoiding Toon Town. But when he takes some compromising pictures of Roger's wife Jessica (Kathleen Turner) with Acme, the stage is set. Acme is murdered, Roger is the prime suspect, and Eddie is the only man who can save him.

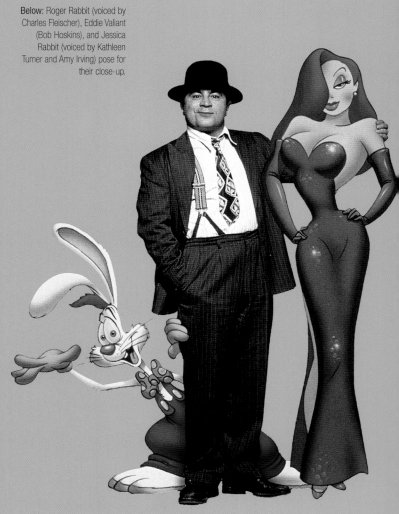

Below: Roger Rabbit (voiced by Charles Fleischer), Eddie Valiant (Bob Hoskins), and Jessica Rabbit (voiced by Kathleen Turner and Amy Irving) pose for their close-up.

The genius of the movie is that Eddie is in a standard noir thriller, or wishes he were, but the characters around him are in a *Silly Symphony* cartoon. While Valiant plays it straight, beyond the requisite hard-boiled one-liners, he's forced to deal with the manic Roger, impossibly hot Jessica, and chain-smokin' Baby Herman. And so he finds himself trapped in an outright farce, thrown across rooms, conked by heavy objects, and handcuffed to a rabbit. Who, of course, could never have been seriously restrained by human means. "Do you mean to tell me you could have taken your hand out of that cuff at any time?" asks the indignant Valiant when Roger shrugs them off. Roger is equally offended. "No, not at any time. Only when it was funny!" That's Eddie's problem: Roger cannot help but react like a 'toon, even if that means blowing his cover when the police are all around.

And then there's Jessica Rabbit, the sexiest film character of all time—not bad, just drawn that way. She's soundtracked that way, too. Her bosom audibly "booiiiings" when it comes into contact with anything, and Kathleen Turner lent her husky voice to the role (Amy Irving handled the singing). The animators poured every fantasy they'd ever had into her dangerous curves, endless legs, and perfectly shadowed eyes to the extent that urban legend has it that, when she's thrown from a cartoon taxicab, it's possible to see scandalous detail under her skirt (if so, you have to *really* want to see it). Finally, Hoskins sells the effect with a stuttering tendency to accidentally look her in the boobs and hastily pull his eyes upward.

Hoskins, in fact, sells the whole thing. His reactions are flawless and the animators matched his every move, using physical effects to be sure that their cartoon characters interact with "reality," whether that's by splashing water, lifting objects, or casting a shadow on the wall. Hoskins reportedly hallucinated cartoon characters for months after the film, exhausted from the effort of imagining Roger and the rest (although Fleischer spent much of the shoot behind camera in a rabbit suit to help him out).

At least, after his recovery, Hoskins had the comfort of knowing it was worth it. The movie was a huge hit at the box office, a critical success, and an enduring masterpiece. Those who turned down the chance to make it (Terry Gilliam, Eddie Murphy, Bill Murray) have gone on record with their regrets. When Hoskins died in 2014, the film was mentioned in the first line of most obituaries. Given this film's enduringly charming combination of human reality and toon magic, that's no discredit to the star.

Below: The innovative mix of animation and live action has rarely been bettered, even decades on.

ORIGINAL RELEASE DATE: June 22, 1988 (U.S.); December 2, 1988 (UK)
RUN TIME: 99 minutes

DID YOU KNOW?

- The book on which the film is based, 1981's *Who Censored Roger Rabbit?*, has two sequels: 1991's *Who P-P-P-Plugged Roger Rabbit?* and 2014's *Who Wacked Roger Rabbit?*

FURTHER VIEWING

- *The Long Good Friday* (1980)
  Bob Hoskins did great work throughout the 1980s, but his finest role comes as a gangster in over his head in this London-set tragedy.

FACTS

BIG

THERE'S A MOMENT TOWARD THE END OF *BIG* WHEN A MIDLEVEL COMEDIC ACTOR REVEALS HIMSELF AS TOM HANKS, THE SOON-TO-BE MOST BELOVED, DOUBLE OSCAR-WINNING MOVIE STAR ON EARTH.

It's all in a look that his character Josh casts back over his shoulder at Elizabeth Perkins's Susan as he walks home, his wish to be "big" over and done. That single look is full of grown-up regret and childish uncertainty that he's doing the right thing, showing a world of knowledge that Josh is not yet ready to process. It's a tiny, lovely moment in a movie that's far more complicated than it's given credit for.

The story is simple, a part of the body-swap/body-morphing tradition established with 1976's original *Freaky Friday* and which also included *Vice Versa*, *Honey I Shrunk the Kids*, *Inner Space*, and another 1988 movie called *14 Going on 30*. Josh Baskin (David Moscow) is twelve years old, on the cusp of his teens and not quite sure whether he's more interested in girls or toy robots. After a particularly frustrating night, when he tries to impress a crush by going on a huge Ferris wheel but finds himself too short to ride, he wishes on a strange fortune-telling machine that he were big. Only, when he wakes up the next morning in an adult body, his horrified mother chases him out of the house and the terrified man-child must make his own way on the mean streets of New York City.

Where the message gets complicated is the fact that Josh makes an unlikely success of his new circumstances. An interest in computing and a few tactical misunderstandings land him an entry-level job at a toy company, and a chance encounter with the boss, when Josh makes a pilgrimage to the legendary New York toy store FAO Schwarz, leads him to rapid promotion, because Josh understands what makes toys work better than his yuppie colleagues ever could.

That toy store scene gives us the moment that everyone remembers, the giant piano duet between Hanks and Robert Loggia's Mr. MacMillan. It's supernaturally charming and works on multiple levels. Josh looks as though he's reveling in how far he can jump in his grown-up lanky frame, but he still focuses seriously on his playing, a conscientious boy practicing his scales. Loggia, meanwhile, delightedly reclaims an unself-conscious sense of play, with a Fred Astaire grace to his stepping that makes it almost a dance.

Then there's the affair between Josh and Susan, the part of the movie that has aged most uncomfortably (particularly when Susan, now aware of Josh's true nature, says, "Maybe in ten or twelve years . . . keep my number"). But even there *Big* somehow treads a line. Susan thinks she can fix this man-child—and for a while it looks like she's right, as Josh strains equally to act the adult (the morning after first having sex, he confidently orders a black coffee from his bemused secretary). His enthusiasms and humor make him self-evidently better than John Heard's awful yuppie competition, and his child-utopia loft apartment is no sillier than any modern tech startup. While a few of his comments should really have given Susan more pause ("Do you mean sleepover? OK, but I get to be on top"—as applied to bunk beds), as painted, it's not obviously creepy. It helps that women don't tend to fetishize teenage boys, something that the gender-swapped almost-remake *13 Going on 30* had to handle more carefully.

What makes the movie unexpectedly meaty and involving, however, is what it quietly says about adulthood. Josh succeeds as an adult precisely because he has the uncynical enthusiasm and barely edited honesty of a child, the very qualities we learn to suppress to become more mature, and shows wisdom beyond either his real or assumed years. His story is a sly commentary on the social mores of adulthood, from the boring suits (Josh arrives at a party in white sparkly tails and explains, "This is a real bow tie, you know; I tied it myself. That's why I was late.") to a dinner party success based around befriending the host's son. Josh looks most childish

when he consciously tries to act like a grown-up. As C. S. Lewis said, "When I became a man I put away childish things, including the fear of childishness and the desire to be very grown up." In the end, Josh's most adult decision is the realization that there is no way to short-circuit growth, and that he has to go back to childhood to become the man he is meant to be. Which, luckily for all of us, turns out to be Tom Hanks.

ORIGINAL RELEASE DATE: June 3, 1988 (U.S.); October 21, 1988 (UK)
RUN TIME: 112 minutes

DID YOU KNOW?

- *Big: The Musical* debuted on Broadway in 1996. It was a costly flop, but after some rewriting the touring version gained good reviews and even played in the UK and Ireland in 2016.

FURTHER VIEWING

- *Dragnet* (1987)
  To see Tom Hanks in all his laddish glory, check him out as the heartthrob partner to Dan Aykroyd's buttoned-up Friday in this straight-faced update of the 1950s TV cop show classic.

FACTS

Opposite: Josh Baskin finds himself newly transformed into his adult self (Tom Hanks) and embarks on a panicked quest to find the fortune-telling machine responsible.

Below: Hanks's Josh and his boss, Mr. MacMillan (Robert Loggia) get their piano practice in on a giant keyboard.

WORKING GIRL

APART FROM THE HAIRSTYLES AND THE FACT THAT
SOMEONE IS TRYING TO BUY A RADIO STATION INSTEAD
OF A STARTUP, *WORKING GIRL* HASN'T AGED A DAY.

Left: Jack (Harrison Ford),
Tess (Melanie Griffith),
and Katharine (Sigourney
Weaver) strike a pose during
a brief pause in their pursuit
of the yuppie dream.

Ambitious strivers are still stymied by richer bosses who take credit for their ideas; toxic offices are still all too prevalent; sexism is still a thing. Few business people look like Melanie Griffith or Harrison Ford, admittedly, but that's about the only thing here that smacks of fantasy, at least until that yuppie fairy-tale ending.

Our (third-billed) heroine is Griffith's Tess, a Staten Island executive assistant who has been studying business in her spare time and working toward a real job on Wall Street. But sexist male bosses have tried to grope and abuse her instead, so when she meets Katharine Parker (Sigourney Weaver), the new boss seems like a dream come true. So much

for appearances. Katharine is a nightmare, stealing Tess's ideas and passing them off as her own. Until, that is, she's incapacitated by a skiing accident and Tess discovers the treachery. Deciding that revenge is a dish best served cold, Tess gets rid of what the *New York Times*'s review called "the hairdo that Farrah Fawcett forgot," takes a meeting with wheeler-dealer Jack Trainer (Ford), and aims to make her own career with the deal.

It's a three-hander of a story, with those stars clicking perfectly under the sure direction of comedy legend Mike Nichols. Ford is taciturn, a little eccentric but quietly funny, prone to changing shirts in the office between meetings (to the delight of his female colleagues—presumably they're *Indiana Jones* fans) and quick to cover for Tess's wilder schemes. Griffith seesaws between wide-eyed innocence and determination in a way that's entirely charming and still relatable. She sets her jaw stubbornly against opposition and soldiers on—still willing to learn from her mistakes but never willing to give up.

But Weaver is the standout: superficially charming, outrageously patronizing, and utterly hissable. Her repeated claims that she and Tess are a "team" and the chummy arm around the shoulders belie her utter ruthlessness in going after whatever she damn well pleases, a model of complete entitlement. She's also hilarious. Explaining why she expects a love interest to propose, she says, "We're in the same city now, I've indicated that I'm receptive to an offer, I've cleared the month of June . . . and I am, after all, me." She sees no "variables" in her scheme, because, after all, who could resist her? Katharine is a serious contender for the most effective villain of the decade, not least because she's the one you're more probable to encounter in the real world. Weaver was nominated for an Oscar as Best Supporting Actress for the role, but the Academy's long-standing hostility to comedic roles might explain her failure to win (her Best Actress nod for *Gorillas in the Mist* in the same year might also have split the Weaver vote).

In today's world, Tess's harassment at the hands of her first boss (Oliver Platt) remains all too familiar ("You don't get ahead in this world by calling your boss a pimp," cautions weary HR officer Olympia Dukakis after Tess protests violently). But this is a film about class more than sexism, blue collar vs. blue blood. The Staten Island–born, night school–educated Tess has had none of the advantages of the wealthy Bostonian Katharine, yet Tess has inspiration and ambition that her wealthier rival lacks. Maybe something more, too, as she claims, "I have a head for business and a bod for sin. Is there anything wrong with that?"

Screenwriter Kevin Wade, who went on to write the Jennifer Lopez vehicle *Maid in Manhattan*, obviously likes an underdog tale, and he and Nichols paint the difference in the two women's worlds

beautifully. Tess's brash friend Cynthia (Joan Cusack) exclaims at Katharine's $6,000 dress that "it's not even leather!" while Alec Baldwin completes the picture as Tess's no-good boyfriend, with greasy hair and cheating ways to burn. This movie has a deep bench of supporting talent. Keep your eyes peeled for Oliver Platt and, if you look hard, a very young David Duchovny.

The moviemaker Nora Ephron said that Nichols made "smart movies about smart people," and this is as strong an example of that tendency as *The Graduate* or any of his work. And it's about a deeply likable smart woman, at that—still an underrepresented demographic on-screen. However much you loathe the Wall Street culture, when Tess takes on the corporate world at its own game and claims her little slice of Manhattan, it's impossible not to cheer.

Below: Katharine prepares to seduce her on-off boyfriend Jack. Despite the outfit, it doesn't quite go to plan.

ORIGINAL RELEASE DATE: December 21, 1988 (U.S.); March 30, 1989 (UK)
RUN TIME: 111 minutes

DID YOU KNOW?

- Carly Simon's theme song, "Let the River Run," won the movie its only Oscar out of six nominations.

FURTHER VIEWING

- *Baby Boom* (1987)
  Diane Keaton plays a stressed executive whose life is thrown for a loop when her late sister leaves her baby in her care.

FACTS

1989 HIGHLIGHTS

The decade closed as it opened, with a Lucasfilm triumph at the box office. But so much else had changed. Steven Soderbergh's win at Cannes was the first shot of the 1990s independent film boom, while Disney Animation recovered its magic and remembered how to make classics . . .

HIGHEST-GROSSING FILMS (U.S.)

1. *Indiana Jones and the Last Crusade*	Paramount Pictures / Lucasfilm	$474,171,806
2. *Batman*	Warner Bros. / PolyGram	$411,348,924
3. *Back to the Future Part II*	Universal Pictures	$331,950,002
4. *Look Who's Talking*	TriStar Pictures	$296,999,813
5. *Dead Poets Society*	Touchstone Pictures	$235,860,116
6. *Lethal Weapon 2*	Warner Bros.	$227,853,986
7. *Honey, I Shrunk the Kids*	Walt Disney Pictures	$222,724,172
8. *Ghostbusters II*	Columbia Pictures	$215,394,738
9. *The Little Mermaid*	Walt Disney Pictures	$184,155,863
10. *Born on the Fourth of July*	Universal Pictures	$161,001,698

AT THE GOLDEN GLOBES

Best Picture (Drama) — *Born on the Fourth of July*

Best Picture (Comedy/Musical) — *Driving Miss Daisy*

Best Director — Oliver Stone, *Born on the Fourth of July*

Best Actor (Drama) — Tom Cruise, *Born on the Fourth of July*

Best Actor (Comedy/Musical) — Morgan Freeman, *Driving Miss Daisy*

Best Actress (Drama) — Michelle Pfeiffer, *The Fabulous Baker Boys*

Best Actress (Comedy/Musical) — Jessica Tandy, *Driving Miss Daisy*

CANNES FILM FESTIVAL

Palme d'Or winner
Sex, Lies and Videotape, Steven Soderbergh

NOTABLE DEATHS

Lucille Ball, April 26 — Actor, *I Love Lucy* and *Dance Girl Dance*

Sergio Leone, April 30 — Director, *Dollars* trilogy and *Once Upon a Time in America*

Mel Blanc, July 10 — Voice actor, *Looney Tunes* and *Who Framed Roger Rabbit*

Laurence Olivier, July 11 — Actor, *Henry V* and *Marathon Man*

Graham Chapman, October 4 — Actor, *The Life of Brian* and *Monty Python and the Holy Grail*

Bette Davis, October 6 — Actor, *Now Voyager* and *Jezebel*

AT THE OSCARS

Best Picture — *Driving Miss Daisy*

Best Director — Oliver Stone, *Born on the Fourth of July*

Best Actor — Daniel Day-Lewis, *My Left Foot*

Best Actress — Jessica Tandy, *Driving Miss Daisy*

THIS YEAR'S BIG OSCARS INJUSTICE

Do the Right Thing and *When Harry Met Sally* receiving a paltry three nominations (and zero wins) between them.

FUTURE MOVIE STAR BIRTHS

February 16: Elizabeth Olsen, *Avengers: Infinity War* and *Wind River*

February 24: Daniel Kaluuya, *Get Out* and *Black Panther*

March 11: Anton Yelchin, *Star Trek* and *Green Room*

June 3: Daniela Vega, *A Fantastic Woman*

July 23: Daniel Radcliffe, *Harry Potter* series and *The Woman in Black*

October 1: Brie Larson, *Short Term 12* and *Captain Marvel*

NOTABLE FILM DEBUTS IN 1989

Vivica A. Fox, *Born on the Fourth of July*

Allison Janney, *Who Shot Patakango?*

Tobey Maguire, *The Wizard*

Sam Rockwell, *Clownhouse*

Adam Sandler, *Going Overboard*

Elijah Wood, *Back to the Future Part II*

HEATHERS

A WILDLY CYNICAL, BLACKLY FUNNY, AND STILL RELEVANT MOVIE ABOUT TEEN ANGST, SUICIDE, AND MURDER?

Left: Heather Chandler (Kim Walker), clipboard in hand, dominates her fellow students, including the other Heathers.

In thirty years, no other teen movie has dared to attempt anything comparable to the trail of death and destruction here, and few movies of any kind have come close to the level of nihilism in this ostensible comedy. *Heathers* flopped in the movie theaters, but it has become a cult classic because it goes against everything we hold dear—or claim that we do.

Writer Dan Waters, in his early twenties, began work on a novel about a girl who meets "the Antichrist as a teenager." He worshipped Stanley Kubrick and considered each of the director's movies the last word on their respective genre. Bored of John Hughes and, more to the point, his imitators, Waters wanted to do the same thing for high-school movies. His answer was *Heathers*, an uncompromising, filthy-minded, dangerous script that was 265 pages long. He sent it to Kubrick and awaited a call that never

came, but in the meantime he showed it to Michael Lehmann, whose student film *Beaver Gets a Boner* was also weird and subversive. Lehmann had notes, chiefly about the length and coherence, and they began to work together. And while the resulting script was too far out for the big studios, producer Denise Di Novi saw its potential and somehow dragged it into production.

Winona Ryder, fifteen years old and fresh from Tim Burton's *Beetlejuice*, campaigned hard for the lead role of Veronica. Veronica is rich, pretty, and smart, but more important, she is one of the Heathers, the clique that rules her school. Heather Chandler (Kim Walker) is the undisputed queen of the gang; Heather McNamara (Lisanne Falk) her cheerleader enabler, and Heather Duke (Shannen Doherty) is their designated whipping girl. Veronica is their useful stooge, an IQ boost for the gang and another tool for Heather Chandler to use in her attempts to take over the world.

And then new boy J.D. (Christian Slater) arrives and strikes up a relationship with Veronica after she has attended a disastrous party at the local college. Veronica is in Heather Chandler's bad books, so she decides to play a trick on the queen bee before her reputation is ruined forever. However, with J.D.'s input, the unpalatable mix that Veronica plans to feed her nemesis is replaced with drain cleaner. Faced with a dead body, this young Bonnie and Clyde fake a suicide note to cover up the crime and try to forget it.

But they can't predict the response. Heather becomes a saint, the whole student body performatively mourning her loss. Then two abusive jocks cross the couple and suffer a similar fate, shot in a staged suicide pact. By now, J.D. has a taste for this mayhem, and she is the only one who can stop him from killing the whole school.

It's a bleak movie. The adults are clueless at best and no help at all. Veronica's parents are relentlessly peppy but fundamentally don't listen; the teachers are hungry for fame or stupid ("Whether to kill yourself or not is one of the most important decisions a teenager can make."); J.D.'s father takes a little too much delight in demolishing buildings as part of his construction business, and J.D. watched his mother walk into one of them in her own suicide. It's dark in other ways, too. At least two Heathers are victims of date rape, and J.D. also attempts to rape Veronica when she tries to break up with him. Our heroine, Veronica, is definitely an accessory to murder if not a murderer herself, and her boyfriend is a true sociopath.

The overall vision of high school life is hellish. Veronica benefits from being one of the popular kids, but she's not constitutionally suited to obeying every edict of Heather Chandler. "It's just like they're people I work with and our job is being popular . . . " explains Veronica. "Maybe it's time to take a vacation," answers J.D. There's hypocrisy as (apparent) suicide transforms bullies into deep, thoughtful martyrs, but when a genuinely tormented girl (Carrie Lynn) tries to take her own

life, she's mocked for it. "Just another case of a geek trying to imitate the popular people at the school and failing miserably," laughs Heather Duke.

This is a 1980s movie that feels more like a 1990s one, with its cynicism more in keeping with that decade's jaundiced eye for conformity and worldly success. It was, inevitably, highly controversial on release and accused of Satanism. Although it opened the door for edgier teen movies such as *Mean Girls*, *Clueless*, and *Election*, there has still been nothing as dark as *Heathers*. As J.D. says, "The extreme always seems to make an impression." How true.

FACTS

ORIGINAL RELEASE DATE:
March 31, 1989 (U.S.); November 17, 1989 (UK)
RUN TIME: 103 minutes

DID YOU KNOW?

◆ Waters had an idea for a sequel in which Veronica is aide to a U.S. senator, played by Meryl Streep, and ends up getting away with the murder of the U.S. president.

FURTHER VIEWING

◆ *The Name of the Rose* (1986)
Christian Slater takes a supporting role alongside Sean Connery in this disturbing literary adaptation about dark goings-on at a medieval monastery under the shadow of the Inquisition.

BATMAN

IT MAY FEEL LIKE MEN IN TIGHTS WERE ALWAYS BOX-OFFICE GOLD, GIVEN THE FLOOD OF SUPERHERO MOVIES TODAY, BUT THAT REALLY ISN'T THE CASE.

While 1978's *Superman* and its first sequel were successful, no movie in the 1980s had successfully capitalized on that first foray into comics, until Tim Burton's 1989 *Batman* was released to spectacular box-office success and a new, more adult tone.

In recent years, the movie has had some grief for not being as dark as Christopher Nolan's *Batman* trilogy, but the 1989 blockbuster was deservedly acclaimed on release. Like Nolan, Burton drew from Frank Miller and Alan Moore's comics work and, casting off the outrageously silly 1960s TV show, took Batman and his foes seriously. The result is a strange blend of 1940s gangster tropes, neo-Gothic cityscapes, and traditional comic book designs. This Gotham is a moody, grimy place that is larger than life, but not impossibly so.

Even in those pre-internet times, the casting of Michael Keaton was initially greeted with horror by fans. A comedian, the Dark Knight? And yet it works. Keaton brings a wry tinge of near self-loathing that defuses the ridiculousness of a man dressing as a bat to fight crime. While he's smart enough to wisecrack with Kim Basinger's photojournalist Vicki Vale and his faithful butler Alfred (Michael Gough), he's also a withdrawn guy who stays removed from the rest of high society.

Above: Even in the Batcave, the Caped Crusader (Michael Keaton) can't find a thing to watch.

However, Jack Nicholson as Jack Napier/the Joker was the real casting coup at the time. He brings theatricality to the chaotic villain, an uneasy mix of crazy and cunning. His Napier is awful long before he falls into a chemical vat and emerges with green hair and a rictus grin (something that gave Nicholson serious muscle ache). His mistress Alicia (Jerry Hall) sees Napier looking in the mirror and assures him, "You look fiiiine." He turns to her, contemptuous: "I didn't ask."

Post-Nolan, some Batman fans claimed that Burton's movie was camp, or cartoony, but there is an edge of random sadism to this Joker that even Heath Ledger's incarnation in *The Dark Knight* didn't match. "I am the world's first fully functional homicidal artist," he claims, after disfiguring Alicia with acid and killing scores of museum visitors in a gas attack. He terrorizes Vicki Vale by threatening self-harm as often as he threatens her directly, and literally burns a rival to a crisp. Cuddly, this is not.

The movie doesn't bother with an origin story—we know who Batman is—and even makes fun of the concept with a fake-out that riffs on the murder of Bruce Wayne's parents. But Burton did make one enduringly controversial choice; here, it is a young Napier who kills the older Waynes, and therefore creates Batman ("You ever dance with the devil in the pale moonlight?" asks Napier). Later, when Batman fails to stop the gangster from falling into a vat of chemical goo, he creates the Joker. That's a neat narrative flourish, and while it outraged comic-book purists (the Joker, they say, should not have a canonical origin, and Batman's parents were killed by a nobody called Joe Chill), it provided an elegant hook for newcomers.

But comic-book blasphemy aside, plenty of choices could come straight from the modern superhero playbook. There's the supporting cast of elder statesmen—Nicholson, Gough, Jack Palance, and Billy Dee Williams—and the (cheap) up-and-comer in the lead role. There is a focus on cool, sometimes over coherence. Burton was even inspired to get Prince to do his soundtrack, a coup that no superhero movie matched until, arguably, *Black Panther*'s Kendrick Lamar soundtrack in 2018.

And it's funny. Robert Wuhl's reporter Alexander Knox, on the trail of stories about a giant vigilante bat, asks, "Is there a six-foot bat in Gotham City? And if so is he on the police payroll? And if so, what's he pullin' down, after taxes?"

It's not a great-looking movie by today's standards, shot in muddy tones and with too many tan suits, but this is now, officially, an underrated *Batman*. Keaton's character is stiff, upright, and a little snarky, but he's also kind of perfect. It may not have been the story that purists wanted, but perhaps this was what they needed to prove to Hollywood that comic-book stories were not just for kids, and could be a box-office gold mine. To quote the World's Greatest Detective himself, "I want you to do me a favor. Tell all your friends about me. I'm Batman."

ORIGINAL RELEASE DATE: June 23, 1989 (U.S.); August 11, 1989 (UK)
RUN TIME: 123 minutes

DID YOU KNOW?

- The Batsuit that Michael Keaton wore didn't let him turn his neck. It also caused him to lose some of his hearing.

FURTHER VIEWING

- *Superman II* (1980)
  The only other comic-book movie of the 1980s that's a must-see, and still the only Superman movie that has truly tested its hero.

FACTS

DO THE RIGHT THING

1989

SPIKE LEE'S THIRD "JOINT" ENDS WITH A DEDICATION TO SIX BLACK NEW YORKERS, FIVE OF WHOM DIED AT THE HANDS OF POLICE, AS WELL AS QUOTES FROM MARTIN LUTHER KING JR. AND MALCOLM X.

It's a blisteringly powerful statement on race and race relations, and it was nominated for a Best Original Screenplay, but snubbed for a Best Picture nomination. *Driving Miss Daisy* won that year, but time has told. Lee's picture remains boilingly relevant while the other film has proven less enduring.

Lee wrote the first draft of his script in two weeks, but it was polished and honed to fit the world he saw and the cast that he assembled. Many of his *School Daze* cast rejoined him, and Lee himself took a leading role as Mookie, while the power of the script—the story of a neighborhood that erupts into violence on the hottest day of the year—brought the rest.

The movie opens with Rosie Perez, intense and focused, dancing up a storm to Public Enemy's "Fight the Power" against red-saturated brownstone housing, inspiring a million 1990s R&B video imitators. The weather is so hot that there is a "jeri-curl alert" in effect ("Stay in the house or you'll end up with a permanent plastic helmet on your head forever," claims Samuel L. Jackson's neighborhood DJ, Mister Señor Love Daddy). Tempers rise along with the temperatures as the day goes on. Lee's challenge to cinematographer Ernest Dickerson, production designer Wynn Thomas, and costume designer Ruth Carter was to make the heat tangible on-screen to the point where Dickerson sometimes held butane lighters directly under the camera in order to create a heat haze.

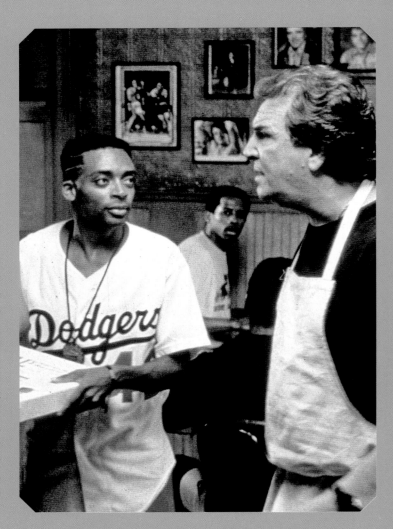

The film was shot on location on Stuyvesant Avenue in Bedford-Stuyvesant, Brooklyn, which Thomas repainted extensively to make the reds and pinks pop and glow. There's a sense of heightened reality, with close and canted angles (inspired by the noir classic *The Third Man*), and an almost theatrical rhythm to the writing, and in the vignettes of everyday life. There's a dueling boombox scene involving Bill Nunn's Radio Raheem, who is inseparable from his music. There are arguments about sports, and Buggin' Out (Giancarlo Esposito) bugs out when a local white man runs over his sneakers with his bike (the culprit is, inevitably, wearing a Larry Bird Celtics shirt).

But the real flash point is the local Italian-owned pizzeria and its owner, Sal (Danny Aiello). Buggin' Out notices, and complains loudly about, the lack of photos of black celebrities on the pizzeria walls. The tension builds, including five direct-to-camera racist tirades against blacks, Italians, and Koreans. Mister Señor Love Daddy calls an end to that interlude, and he later reels off a list of major black artists and thinkers, giving the movie extra appeal as a cultural primer. Buggin' then tries to organize a boycott of Sal's Famous Pizzeria ("Black Panther eat pizza! We eat pizza, booiiiii!" objects one of his would-be recruits), but his plan goes wrong.

This is a movie that portrays prejudice, racism, and anger—righteous, furious anger—but it's not a simple story. Sal and his sons are not entirely unsympathetic; Sal is trying to do right by a neighborhood where he is in the minority, but when he does lose his temper, he resorts to racist insults as a default. The older man whales on Raheem's boom box and is attacked by not only Raheem but also even the mentally disabled Smiley (Roger Guenveur Smith). And when the cops show up, they take Raheem and choke him to death. It's hard to watch, but it was not unprecedented even in 1989; Lee and his team considered the film a depiction of their reality and were surprised that it proved at all controversial.

It's Mookie who then throws the first object through the pizzeria's windows. There's a fair argument that he was trying to distract the crowd

ORIGINAL RELEASE DATE: July 21, 1989 (U.S.); June 23, 1989 (UK)
RUN TIME: 115 minutes

DID YOU KNOW?

- This was the first movie for both Martin Lawrence and Rosie Perez.

FURTHER VIEWING

- *She's Gotta Have It* (1986)
  Spike Lee's debut movie is uneasy viewing in its depiction of rape, but it was groundbreaking in portraying a sexually liberated African American woman and her refusal to embrace monogamy.

FACTS

away from Sal and toward Sal's property to save the man's life. But he is angry, too, justifiably so, and maybe he just did it to let the anger out. Lee doesn't offer easy answers here, but he does paint a picture of a recognizable, flawed America full of people just trying to do the right thing.

As the smoke clears the next morning, Love Daddy on the radio offers that "Today, the cash money word is chill," and it seems like a note of hope. But he also tells his listeners to register to vote, and the final dedication is a song for Radio Raheem. If there is a message in *Do the Right Thing*, it is that one should love where possible, stay calm where possible, but do not relax and do not forget.

Opposite: Lee has taken on acting roles in several of his films, including *Do the Right Thing*.

Below: The racial tensions on show in *Do the Right Thing* are, sadly, more relevant than ever today.

THE LITTLE MERMAID

1989

IN THE MID-1980S, WALT DISNEY ANIMATION WAS DEAD ON ITS FEET.

The old guard, Disney's "Nine Old Men," were retired or retiring. New talent, including Tim Burton and Pixar founder John Lasseter, left the moribund studio in frustration at the hidebound executives who replaced those giants, and the glory days seemed to be over. And then came *The Little Mermaid*, and a return to form that has propelled the studio through three more decades of megahits.

As with most feature animation fairy tales, the notion of filming the Hans Christian Andersen classic floated around for decades before someone finally found a way to make it work. Ron Clements and John Musker were already veterans of one of the few mid-1980s hits for the studio, *The Great Mouse Detective*,

when they pitched for a new take on *The Little Mermaid* story in 1986. It would be a return to the classic fairy tales that had built Disney, but with a smarter, more intrepid princess than the smiling blanks of old, and it would be made on an epic scale using brand-new computer animation as well as traditional techniques, sucking up almost all the animation resources at the studio. Some of the work was done even farther afield: animators in China were responsible for the movie's million-or-so bubbles. The film was nearly delayed by the unrest following the Tiananmen Square massacre in June 1989, when all the finished bubble cells were locked in a vault in anticipation of possible civil war.

Below: Ariel (Jodi Benson) horses around with sea horses during one of *The Little Mermaid*'s big musical numbers, "Under the Sea."

Opposite: Ariel argues with self-important crab Sebastian (Samuel E. Wright) and her lovable sidekick Flounder (Jason Marin).

Eventually the violence ended and the bubbles were shipped home to Disney.

That moment in production was the only intrusion of bleak reality into a movie that builds a fantastical world seamlessly around its diminutive heroine. The tone was something new, faster and funnier than what the studio had done before, but it was also rooted in traditional Disney strengths: fairy tales, princesses, and the triumph of true love. Musker and Clements took note of Walt Disney's greatest hits and freely adopted the parts that worked to give the movie that classical Disney feel. So there were animal sidekicks, just as in *Cinderella* and *Snow White*. But this time, particularly in the case of crab composer Sebastian (Samuel E. Wright), they were sassier and funnier than before to compensate for their mostly voiceless heroine. The directors kept to the gist of the story, where a mermaid falls in love with a human and gives up her voice for legs, but they stripped away Andersen's more sadistic flourishes (in the fairy tale, every step is like walking on knives) in favor of Disney bombast (that gigantic finale). They made Prince Eric (Joshua Finkel) a total babe and an adventurer, so we could understand the intrepid Ariel's (Jodi Benson) crush on him. Perhaps most important of all, they brought in two off-Broadway mavericks, composer Alan Menken and lyricist Howard Ashman, to make the movie sing.

The creators of the horror-comedy rock musical *Little Shop of Horrors* might not have seemed like a natural fit for Disney, but the match worked. Menken's gorgeous, catchy tunes gave the story heart and kept up the pace, while Ashman added wit and attitude, and just a touch of cynicism. Their success was immediate, although the scale of their achievement took a little longer to become clear. By 1995, the Academy actually changed the Oscar rules following Menken's eight wins and twelve nominations for Best Song and Best Score with Disney movies to give other composers a chance (he's had a mere six nominations in the years since).

Musker and Clements made creative room for a new generation of animation geniuses at Disney Animation (Glen Keane, Mark Henn, Andreas Deja, etc.), and they rose to meet the challenge, creating a

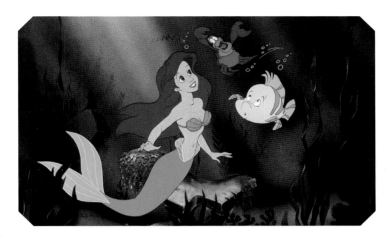

dazzling underwater world, a gorgeous heroine, and, in the sea witch Ursula (Pat Carroll), their best villain since Maleficent. There were magnificent storms at sea, big musical numbers, and more fish than a French marketplace. It felt like a Disney classic, even on release, with none of the compromise or creative conservatism that marked movies such as *The Black Cauldron* or *Oliver & Company*.

Initially, *The Little Mermaid* was a solid rather than runaway success at the box office, but it had serious legs on home video and, more important, it showed that Disney was back. Their next effort, 1991's *Beauty and the Beast*, would become the first animated film ever nominated for Best Picture at the Oscars, and a string of successes—*Aladdin*, *The Lion King*—would follow into the mid-1990s and beyond. But the magic began, again, with *Mermaid* and its fairy-tale vision of what Disney had been, and should remain.

ORIGINAL RELEASE DATE: November 17, 1989 (U.S.); October 12, 1990 (UK)
RUN TIME: 85 minutes

DID YOU KNOW?
- A pre-megastardom Jim Carrey was one of the people who auditioned to play Prince Eric.

FURTHER VIEWING
- *Little Shop of Horrors* (1986)
  This classic has Rick Moranis and Ellen Green leading a star-studded adaptation of Menken and Ashman's twisted hit about a man-eating plant in 1950s New York.

FACTS

WHEN HARRY MET SALLY

THERE ARE FEW ROMANTIC COMEDIES THAT EVERYONE ALLOWS THEMSELVES TO LIKE.

Left: The story is a charming one, but the movie soars thanks to the chemistry and comic ability of Billy Crystal and Meg Ryan.

Annie Hall is one, acceptable chiefly because of its downbeat ending, and *When Harry Met Sally* is another, because even grumps can't deny that it's one of the smartest and funniest movies of the decade. Impeccably cast with Billy Crystal and Meg Ryan in the title roles, it half-heartedly discusses the idea of whether straight men and women can ever truly be friends, but really plays out as a drawn-out romance between two people who are surprisingly perfect for each other.

It all began with director Rob Reiner, who had recently become single after his marriage broke down. He was struggling to re-enter the dating world when he met up with writer Nora Ephron to discuss a film project with her. She hated the idea that was put to her, but liked Reiner, and they began to work on a concept about modern dating. Their experiences and personalities informed the two characters. Reiner was bereft after the breakdown of his marriage ("He was depressed, but he was very fond of his depression. His depression . . . was like a pet he would trot out and make jokes about," said Ephron), and that became a key part of Harry's story. The big emotional discussion between Harry and his best friend Jess (Bruno Kirby) during a Mexican wave at a baseball game really happened to Reiner and a buddy; he even used to lie there and moan at night, like Harry.

Sally's overly complicated method of ordering food and drink came straight from Ephron ("Regular tomato juice, filled up about three-quarters, then a splash of Bloody Mary mix but just a splash, and a slice of lime on the side"), as did her pose of emotional control at all times. She also contributed what became a key scene. She and Reiner felt that Sally was hit with a lot of unwelcome revelations about men, but Harry had not been thrown out of his comfort zone in the same way, so she suggested the key scene where Harry learns that most women fake orgasms at some point in their lives. That led to the scene where Sally demonstrates the skill in a crowded restaurant (Katz's Deli), and Reiner's mother Estelle played the customer who caps the scene by telling a waitress, "I'll have what she's having."

This is a movie almost entirely without incident; the closest thing we get to an action scene is Harry running to a party toward the end. It's a movie about people talking in cars, and apartments, and restaurants. Sally and her best friend Marie (Carrie Fisher) go for a meal and discuss Marie's ill-judged affairs ("He's never going to leave her."). Even when they're in different parts of town, the movie uses a split screen to show people talking on the phone—something modeled on Reiner and Crystal, real-life friends who would lie in their respective beds chatting—because the talking is what matters. With dialogue as good as Ephron's, it makes sense that the words would be front and center. Or the words, and New York—because Harry and Sally's walks take them through Central Park in fall, and the Metropolitan Museum, and Washington Square, and make the city look magical.

But it all hangs on Crystal and Ryan. He's at his most sardonic and self-deprecating, contributing some of the film's best moments through improv and suggestion. And she is adorable, clever, weird, and funny. "I have just as much of a dark side as the next person!" she says, with her Farrah Fawcett hair and bright smile. Harry doesn't believe her, of course, but then their dynamic involves each of them calling the other out. She turns from laughter to tears on a dime, he turns from caring friend to man desperate to escape after sex almost as fast.

"Most of the time, when you fall in love with someone, it's not after a long, long friendship that doesn't involve sex," claimed Ephron, so the first couple of drafts didn't have Harry and Sally end up together, which seemed more honest to Ephron. But it didn't work. Perhaps movies demand a happy ending, or perhaps it became clear that these two are too smart and strange for anyone else. Or perhaps art was reflecting life: Reiner met his second wife, Michele Singer, during the making of the movie and fell in love again. And so Harry, too, takes a leap of faith and dares to declare love. As Fisher says, "I don't want to be cynical about this stuff. I am, most of the time, but I'm happiest when I'm hopeful." *When Harry Met Sally* gives us all hope.

Below: Sally (Ryan) proving the acting abilities that she claimed all women possess.

INDEX

CREDITS

Special thank you to REX/Shutterstock, who kindly supplied photographs with the exception of page 34 (Alamy/Editorial)

104; /20th Century Fox/Allied Stars/Enigma/Kobal: 12-13, 41; /20th Century Fox/Kobal: 28, 70r, 100, 101, 121, 122, 124, 125, 130, 131, 132, 144, 158, 159; / Amblin Entertainment/Universal Pictures/Kobal: 86t, 86b, 137; /Cannon/Kobal: 104tr; /Castle Rock/Nelson/Columbia/KobalL 170, 171; /Columbia/Kobal: 54, 55, 68, 69, 70l, 82, 83, 106, 107; /Cristaldifilm/Films Ariane/Kobal: 153t; /De Laurentiis/Kobal: 103tl; /Gracie/Kobal: 136; /Brian Hamill/20th Century Fox/ Kobal: 156, 157; /Harms/AP: 71l; /Herald Ace/Nippon Herald/Greenwich/Kobal: 151; /ITV: 30, 58l; /Kobal: 91br, 92bl, 92br; /Ladd Company/Warner Bros: 50, 51; / Lucasfilm/Fox/Kobal: 10-11, 16, 18, 19; /Lucasfilm Ltd/Paramount/Kobal: 32, 33; / Jim Henson Productions/Kobal: 116, 117; /Lynne McAfee: 71b; /Bruce McBroom/ Universal/Kobal: 44r; /Sam Emerson/Ultimate Prods./Kobal: 81; /MGM/Kobal: 71cl; /MGM/UA/Kobal: 149; /Moviestore Collection: 14, 22, 42, 48, 49, 58r, 71cr, 78, 80, 96r, 103br. 104br, 105, 112, 114, 115, 127, 128, 134, 135, 146, 147, 148, 152t, 153l, 153b, 166; /New Line/The Elm Street Venture/Kobal: 79; /Jane O'Neal/ Warner Bros/Kobal: 140; /Optimus Prods/Kobal: 35; /Orion/Kobal: 64t, 64b, 65, 66, 96l; /Paragon/Golden Harvest/Kobal: 104tl; /Paramount/Kobal: 8-9, 11t, 26, 27, 52, 53, 70r, 74, 75, 92tl, 98, 99, 108, 109, 110, 113, 129; /Renaissance/Kobal: 60, 61; /Bonnie Schiffman/Touchstone/Kobal: 118; /Andy Schwartz/20th Century Fox/Kobal: 120; /Sipa Press: 70bl; /Snap: 38, 40, 43, 71tr, 102, 104bl, 126, 152b, 160, 162, 163, 168, 169; /Peter Sorel/20th Century Fox/Kobal: 11b, 103bl, 145; /Spinal Tap Production/Kobal: 76, 77; /Studio Ghibli/Kobal: 150; /Touchstone/ Kobal: 62; /Touchstone/Amblin/Kobal: 154, 155; /Unimedia International: 37; / United Artists/Kobal: 103tr; /Universal/Kobal: 15, 20, 21, 44l, 45, 56, 57, 84, 90, 91tl, 91tr, 91bl, 92tr, 94, 167, 176/ Vestron/Kobal: 138, 139; /Warner Bros/Kobal: 36, 72, 73, 88, 89, 141, 142; /Warner Bros/DC Comics/Kobal: 164, 165